*DESPERTARSE - The Unstoppable You*

**OrangeBooks Publication**

1st Floor, Rajhans Arcade, Mall Road, Kohka, Bhilai, Chhattisgarh 490020

Website: **www.orangebooks.in**

---



**First Edition, 2026**

**ISBN:** 978-93-7426-522-2

**Price:** Rs. 350.00



Printed in India

# DESPERTARSE
# THE UNSTOPPABLE YOU

A JOURNEY TO SELF-MASTERY, PURPOSE,
AND UNLIMITED POTENTIAL

BARUN MONDAL

OrangeBooks Publication
www.orangebooks.in

# Contents

## Part One

The Foundation of Transformation

# DESPERTARSE- The Unstoppable You

*A Journey to Self-Mastery, Purpose, and Unlimited Potential*

**By Barun Mondal**

## INTRODUCTION: THE POWER WITHIN

You hold in your hands more than just a book. This is a mirror reflecting the person you are capable of becoming—the unstoppable force that lies dormant within you, waiting to be awakened. Every page you turn is a step closer to the extraordinary life that destiny has prepared for you.

For too long, you may have believed that success, happiness, and fulfillment were reserved for others—the talented, the lucky, the privileged. But I am here to shatter that illusion and reveal a truth that has transformed millions of lives: **Your thoughts create your reality. Your attitude determines your altitude. Your mind is the most powerful tool you possess.**

This book synthesizes the wisdom of the greatest self-development minds of our time. It combines the subconscious programming principles of Joseph Murphy, the attitude transformation insights of Jeff Keller, the grit and perseverance philosophy of Angela Duckworth, the present-moment awareness of Eckhart Tolle, and the relationship mastery of Dale Carnegie. Together, these principles form a comprehensive roadmap to self-mastery.

Over the next chapters, you will discover:

- How to reprogram your subconscious mind for success
- The art of maintaining an unshakeable positive attitude
- Strategies to overcome resistance and self-sabotage
- The power of grit in achieving long-term goals
- Techniques for building meaningful relationships

- Methods for living in the present moment

- The practice of self-acceptance and wholehearted living

Your transformation begins now. The mountain before you is not external—it is the internal barriers, limiting beliefs, and fears that have held you back. This book will guide you to climb that mountain and discover that the summit was within you all along.

Are you ready to awaken the unstoppable you?

# PART ONE: THE FOUNDATION OF TRANSFORMATION

# CHAPTER 1: THE POWER OF YOUR SUBCONSCIOUS MIND

## The Two Minds That Shape Your Destiny

Inside you live two extraordinary minds: the **conscious** and the **subconscious**.
The conscious mind is your captain — it reasons, plans, analyzes, and decides.
The subconscious mind is your crew — silent, loyal, and unimaginably powerful. Whatever the captain commands, the crew obeys.

Every thought you think is a seed, and your subconscious is the soil. Whatever you plant in it, it will grow — whether that seed is one of confidence and abundance or doubt and limitation.

Most people live as prisoners of unconscious programming. They wonder why life keeps repeating the same patterns — financial struggles, toxic relationships, unfulfilled dreams — without realizing that their subconscious mind is simply executing the instructions they unknowingly gave it years ago.

If you constantly think, *"I'm not good enough,"* your subconscious accepts that as truth and ensures you act, speak, and choose in ways that prove it. But if you affirm, *"I am capable, confident, and worthy of success,"* your subconscious will rearrange your perception and actions to make that true as well.

Your subconscious doesn't judge or question — it simply obeys.
That's both your greatest danger and your greatest opportunity.

### The Law of Belief

There is one governing law that shapes every human experience: **the Law of Belief**.
Whatever you believe with emotion and repetition becomes your reality.

You can only receive what you truly believe is possible.
If you believe money is scarce, it will be scarce. If you believe success requires suffering, you'll unconsciously make sure it does. If you believe you can achieve greatness, the universe will conspire to help you do it.

Beliefs are not inherited truths — they're learned stories, and every story can be rewritten.
The moment you change your belief, you change your destiny.

**Programming the Subconscious**

The subconscious mind learns through **repetition, emotion, and imagery**.
Let's explore the core methods to reprogram it:

**1. Autosuggestion and Affirmations**

Affirmations are statements of truth that you feed your subconscious until it accepts them as reality. The key is **emotion**. Words without feeling are like seeds on concrete — they never take root.

Each morning and night, repeat affirmations like:

- "I am confident and capable in every situation."
- "Abundance flows to me easily and consistently."
- "I am healthy, vibrant, and full of energy."
- "I attract supportive, positive people into my life."

Say them slowly, feel them deeply, and visualize their truth. Imagine how life feels when these statements are already real.

**2. Visualization**

Your subconscious doesn't distinguish between a vividly imagined scene and a real one. That's why visualization is so powerful.

Every night before sleep, create a mental movie of your success.
See yourself walking into your dream job, speaking confidently on stage, or waking up in your new home.
Feel the joy, the excitement, the gratitude as though it's happening now.

If you hold that image with enough emotion and consistency, your subconscious will begin aligning circumstances, opportunities, and even people to make it real.

**3. The Gratitude Practice**

Gratitude is a magnet for miracles. It tells your subconscious, *"I already have what I desire."* And since the subconscious always works to make your dominant thoughts true, it brings you more of what you feel grateful for.

Each morning, write down five things you're grateful for — some from your current reality, some from your desired future.
For example:

- "I am grateful for the meaningful work I do."
- "I am grateful for my strong, healthy body."
- "I am grateful for the peace and confidence guiding my day."

When you practice gratitude with emotion, you open the floodgates of abundance.

**4. Mental Rehearsal Before Sleep**

The moments before sleep are sacred. Your brain transitions from conscious to subconscious dominance — the perfect time for reprogramming.

Instead of replaying worries, visualize success.
If you have a presentation, imagine yourself speaking with clarity and confidence.

If you have an exam or interview, see yourself calm, prepared, and successful.

Your subconscious will spend the night working toward the picture you give it.

**Overcoming Negative Programming**

Many of your limiting beliefs were not chosen — they were *inherited*.
Perhaps you grew up hearing, "Money doesn't grow on trees," or "People like us don't get ahead."
Without realizing it, you accepted those statements as truth, and they became self-fulfilling prophecies.

But here's the liberating truth:
You are not the voice in your head — you are the one who *hears* it.
And that means you have the power to change it.

When you catch yourself thinking, "I can't," immediately replace it with, "I'm learning."
When you think, "I'll never be successful," replace it with, "Every day, I'm moving closer to success."
Each correction is a small act of self-leadership — a signal to your subconscious that you're taking charge.

You are the programmer. Your mind is the software. Your thoughts are the code.

**The Infinite Intelligence Within**

Your subconscious is not limited to your personal mind — it's connected to **Infinite Intelligence**, the universal consciousness that orchestrates life itself.

When you align your beliefs with this higher intelligence, you access creativity, guidance, and solutions beyond logic.
Before sleep, ask your subconscious powerful questions:

- "What's the best way to solve this challenge?"

- "What's my next step toward my goal?"

Then trust that the answer will come — through intuition, a conversation, or a sudden flash of inspiration. The universe always responds to a focused, faithful mind.

**The Healing Power of the Subconscious**

Your subconscious governs all vital functions — heartbeat, digestion, immunity, cellular repair. It already knows how to heal you.
When you affirm, *"Every cell in my body radiates vitality and health,"* you're speaking directly to your body's intelligence.

Science continues to confirm the mind-body connection: thoughts of peace and gratitude strengthen your immune system, while chronic stress suppresses it.
When you align your mental and emotional state with harmony, your body follows.

**Your Thoughts Are Things**

Everything you experience — your career, relationships, health — is the result of consistent thought patterns. Your thoughts are **causes**, and your life conditions are **effects**.
To change the effects, you must change the causes.

This isn't about blame — it's about power. You may not control everything that happens, but you always control your response, your meaning, and your mindset.

If you want new results, start thinking new thoughts.

---

### REFLECTION QUESTIONS

1. What are three recurring thoughts I notice about myself or my abilities?
2. How have these thoughts shaped my current reality?
3. What new empowering beliefs do I want to program into my subconscious?

### AFFIRMATIONS FOR REPROGRAMMING

- My mind is a powerful creator, and I choose thoughts that uplift and empower me.
- I am aligned with infinite intelligence, and solutions flow to me easily.
- Every day, I am becoming the person I was meant to be.

### PRACTICAL ACTION STEPS

1. Write your top five affirmations and place them where you'll see them often — mirror, phone screen, or journal.
2. Each night, visualize one goal as already achieved and feel the gratitude of its fulfillment.
3. Start a "Gratitude Journal" and record five things daily — including dreams you're calling into reality.

---

# CHAPTER 2: ATTITUDE IS EVERYTHING

## Your Attitude Is the Lens of Your Life

If your subconscious mind is the engine of your destiny, your **attitude** is the steering wheel. It determines the direction in which that powerful engine will take you.

Your attitude is how you interpret life — it's the lens through which you view every experience. When the lens is clean and clear, the world appears full of possibility, hope, and opportunity. But when the lens is clouded with negativity, fear, and self-pity, even the brightest moments look dull.

Here's the truth most people never realize: **Your attitude is not shaped by your circumstances — your circumstances are shaped by your attitude.**

Two people can experience the same setback — a job loss, a rejection, a breakup — and interpret it in completely different ways. One sees it as the end of the road. The other sees it as a redirection toward something better. The difference between them isn't luck or talent — it's *attitude*.

The good news? Attitude is a **choice**, not a fixed trait. You can't always control what happens to you, but you can always control how you respond. And that single decision — to choose your response — holds the power to change everything.

---

## The Hidden Power of Perspective

There's an old saying: "You can't choose the cards you're dealt, but you can choose how to play your hand."

Life will deal you both triumphs and trials. The way you *frame* those experiences determines whether you grow or stay stuck.

Think of your attitude as a thermostat, not a thermometer. A thermometer merely reflects the temperature of its environment — it reacts. A thermostat, on the other hand, sets the temperature — it influences.

When you let your external conditions dictate your mood, you're living like a thermometer — reacting to whatever happens. But when you set your internal state intentionally — choosing optimism, faith, and gratitude — you're living like a thermostat. You regulate your world from the inside out.

When you reach that level of mastery, challenges no longer define you — they refine you.

---

**The Science of Attitude**

Psychologists have long known that attitude impacts not only success, but health, relationships, and even longevity. Studies show that optimistic people recover faster from illness, earn higher income, perform better under stress, and build stronger relationships.

Why? Because optimism expands your awareness. When you expect good things, your brain literally opens up — you notice more options, think more creatively, and act more decisively.

Negativity, on the other hand, narrows your focus. When you dwell on fear or frustration, your brain enters survival mode. It shuts down creativity, empathy, and long-term thinking. You can't see opportunity because you're too busy scanning for threats.

This is why two people can face the same situation, yet on
ly one thrives— their internal state determines what they're capable of perceiving and acting upon.

As motivational speaker Zig Ziglar said, *"Your attitude, not your aptitude, determines your altitude."*

## The Characteristics of a Winning Attitude

So, what separates those who thrive from those who barely survive? There are five core characteristics shared by people with unstoppable attitudes. Let's explore each one.

### 1. Enthusiasm – The Spark That Ignites Action

Enthusiasm is the emotional fuel of success. It's not about forced excitement — it's the natural energy that comes from believing in what you're doing.

When you speak with enthusiasm, people listen. When you work with enthusiasm, opportunities notice you. When you live with enthusiasm, life opens doors that were previously invisible.

You've met people who radiate this kind of energy — they light up a room simply by being there. That's not luck; that's attitude.

If you've lost touch with enthusiasm, don't wait for life to excite you again— *choose* to reignite it. Focus on what's meaningful. Engage in work that matters. Look for the spark in every situation — and if you can't find one, bring your own.

### 2. Optimism – Seeing Possibility in the Impossible

Optimism isn't denial of reality — it's the decision to focus on potential rather than limitation.

When faced with a setback, pessimists ask, "Why is this happening to me?"
Optimists ask, "What can I learn from this?"

That single question transforms victimhood into growth.

Optimism doesn't mean everything always works out as you wish; it means you believe that, no matter what happens, *you will find a way to grow through it.*

Practice catching your pessimistic thoughts and flipping them.
Instead of "This is too hard," say, "This is a challenge that will make me stronger."
Instead of "I failed," say, "I learned what doesn't work — and now I'm closer to what will."

**3. Resilience – The Art of Rising Again**

Resilience is your ability to bounce back when life knocks you down — and it *will* knock you down. Everyone gets punched by reality at some point. The difference is that some people stay down, while others get back up, dust off, and keep moving forward.

Thomas Edison failed more than a thousand times before perfecting the light bulb. When asked how he dealt with failure, he said, "I didn't fail a thousand times — I discovered a thousand ways that don't work."

Resilience isn't something you're born with — it's something you build by refusing to quit. Every time you recover from disappointment, you become a little stronger, a little wiser, a little tougher.

Each challenge you overcome becomes evidence that you can handle the next one.

**4. Responsibility – Owning Your Power**

When you stop blaming others, you reclaim your power.

It's easy to say, "I'd be happy if my boss were better," or "I'd be successful if the economy were different." But those statements make you powerless. The moment you take responsibility — for your choices, your attitude, and your results — you step into your personal power.

Responsibility is not about guilt or blame; it's about ownership. It's realizing that while you can't control everything that happens, you always control how you interpret and respond to it.

Winners don't say, "It's not my fault." They say, "It's my life, and I choose how to shape it."

### 5. Self-Discipline – Doing What Needs to Be Done

Success doesn't come from occasional bursts of motivation; it comes from consistent action, even when you don't feel like it. That's self-discipline.

Self-discipline is the muscle that turns dreams into reality. It's what gets you out of bed early to exercise, keeps you focused when distractions call, and pushes you to finish what you start.

Each time you keep a promise to yourself, you strengthen your discipline muscle. Start small. Show up daily. Over time, consistency compounds into mastery.

#### The Morning Attitude Reset

Every morning, you're given a blank page — a new opportunity to set the tone for your day. The first few minutes after you wake up are sacred; they determine your mental state for hours.

Try this morning ritual:

1. **Gratitude:** Before your feet hit the floor, say three things you're grateful for.

2. **Affirmation:** Speak one empowering statement aloud: "Today, I choose positivity and progress."

3. **Movement:** Stretch, walk, or exercise — physical energy fuels mental clarity.

4. **Intention:** Ask, "How do I want to show up today?"

This simple practice transforms your mornings from autopilot to intention. Instead of being swept away by stress, you start each day steering your own ship.

**The Power of Your Words**

Your words shape your world. Every sentence you speak is an affirmation — either empowering or disempowering.

When you say, "I'm so stressed," you're programming stress.
When you say, "I can handle this calmly," you're programming resilience.

Start paying attention to your language. Replace "I have to" with "I get to."
"I have to go to work" becomes "I get to contribute and grow today."
"I have to study" becomes "I get to learn something that expands my potential."

Small linguistic shifts create massive mental shifts.

---

**The Company You Keep**

Your attitude is contagious — and so is everyone else's.

If you spend time with complainers, cynics, or people who constantly focus on problems, their energy will infect yours. On the other hand, when you surround yourself with positive, ambitious, and growth-oriented people, your standards rise.

Jim Rohn famously said, "You are the average of the five people you spend the most time with."
Take a look at your circle. Do they inspire you or drain you? Do they challenge you or comfort your excuses?

Surround yourself with people who make you better — who celebrate your growth, not your gossip.

---

### The Silver Lining Mindset

There's a secret to maintaining an unshakable attitude: **look for the gift in every situation.**

Lost a job? Maybe it's the universe redirecting you to a better career.
A relationship ended? Perhaps it's clearing space for a healthier connection.
A plan failed? Maybe it was never meant to succeed — it was meant to teach.

When you consciously search for meaning in adversity, pain transforms into purpose. You stop asking "Why me?" and start asking "What is this trying to teach me?"

The people who grow the most aren't those who avoid pain — they're the ones who use pain as fuel for evolution.

---

### The Commitment Factor

A positive attitude is powerful, but it's not enough without commitment. You must decide — deeply and fully — that no matter what challenges arise, you will keep going.

Commitment is the point of no return. It's the moment you say, *"I'm all in."*

When you commit fully, the universe rearranges itself to meet your determination. Opportunities appear. Resources emerge. People show up.

It's not magic — it's alignment. The world responds to unwavering energy.

---

**Taking Massive Action**

A great attitude without action is like a car in neutral — full of potential but going nowhere.

Take the first step, even if it's small. You don't need to have the whole path figured out; you just need momentum. Every action, however small, builds confidence.

Don't wait for the perfect time. Start before you're ready. Act boldly, learn as you go, and let your attitude carry you forward.

---

**REFLECTION QUESTIONS**

1. How do I usually respond when things don't go as planned?
2. Which of the five attitude characteristics (enthusiasm, optimism, resilience, responsibility, self-discipline) do I most need to strengthen right now?
3. Who are the five people I spend the most time with, and how do they influence my mindset?

**AFFIRMATIONS FOR REPROGRAMMING**

- I choose my attitude, and my attitude creates my world.
- I see opportunities where others see obstacles.
- Every challenge I face makes me stronger, wiser, and more resilient.

**PRACTICAL ACTION STEPS**

1. Each morning, complete the 4-step "Attitude Reset" ritual before checking your phone.
2. Journal nightly about one situation where you consciously chose a positive perspective.
3. Identify one negative influence in your environment and replace it with a positive one — a book, podcast, or person who uplifts your energy.

# CHAPTER 3: DOPAMINE DETOX — RECLAIMING YOUR FOCUS

### The Silent Epidemic of Distraction

There's a quiet epidemic spreading across the world — one that doesn't make headlines, yet touches nearly every mind and home. It's not a virus or a disease. It's **distraction**.

We live in an age where our attention — once our most sacred resource— has become the world's most traded commodity. Every ping, notification, scroll, and alert is a little tug at your consciousness, pulling you away from presence and purpose.

Think about it: How often do you reach for your phone the moment you wake up? How many times a day do you check your messages, not because there's something urgent, but because your brain whispers, *"Maybe there's something new..."*?

We've become so addicted to stimulation that silence now feels uncomfortable. We've trained our brains to crave constant novelty — a never-ending flood of digital sugar hits that keep us busy but empty.

The result? Fragmented attention, shallow focus, anxiety, and a constant sense of restlessness. You may feel like you're doing a lot, but deep down, you know you're not truly moving forward.

It's not your fault — your brain is doing exactly what it was designed to do.

---

### Understanding Dopamine: The Brain's Reward Chemical

To reclaim your focus, you first need to understand **dopamine** — the molecule behind motivation, pleasure, and reward.

Dopamine isn't inherently bad. In fact, it's what drives you to pursue goals, complete tasks, and grow. Every time you make progress toward something meaningful, your brain releases dopamine, making you feel good and reinforcing that behavior.

But here's the problem:
The modern world has hijacked this system.

Social media likes, notifications, endless video reels, junk food, shopping, and even the constant flood of news — all of these are engineered to release short bursts of dopamine. Your brain starts to associate these quick hits with reward, while meaningful, long-term activities — like reading, studying, building a business, or meditating — feel dull in comparison.

Over time, your brain becomes **desensitized**. You need more stimulation to feel the same satisfaction. This creates the cycle of *dopamine dependency* — where you're always seeking something new, but never feeling fulfilled.

You may think, *"I'm just scrolling for a few minutes,"* but what's really happening is that you're training your brain to expect instant gratification and to avoid anything that requires patience or deep effort.

---

**The High-Cost of Overstimulation**

Let's be honest — we've all felt it.

You sit down to work on something important, but somehow end up on YouTube. You plan to read a book, but check your phone "just for a second." You open one tab to research a topic, and suddenly you're fifteen tabs deep into unrelated videos or articles.

Each of those moments steals a piece of your focus, and it takes an average of **23 minutes** to regain full concentration after a single distraction. That means if you get interrupted every 10 minutes, you never truly enter a deep, productive state.

And here's the more dangerous part — this constant switching fragments your ability to think deeply, plan strategically, and create meaningfully.

You start craving stimulation the way an addict craves a fix. You can't sit quietly anymore. You reach for your phone at red lights, during meals, or even in moments of peace.

You might not realize it, but your brain is slowly losing its ability to experience satisfaction from simple, slow, and profound experiences — like reading, creating, or reflecting.

That's the hidden cost of overstimulation:

- You become restless even in calm.
- You lose patience for meaningful work.
- You feel exhausted, even after doing nothing.

The very tools designed to connect us are disconnecting us — from our focus, our purpose, and ourselves.

---

**The Dopamine Detox: Resetting Your Brain**

The solution is not to eliminate dopamine — that would be impossible and unhealthy. The solution is to **reset your dopamine balance**, to give your brain a chance to recalibrate and rediscover joy in the slow, meaningful things again.

This process is called a **Dopamine Detox** — a term popularized by productivity experts like Thibaut Meurisse and Dr. Cameron Sepah.

A dopamine detox is a short period during which you intentionally reduce exposure to high-dopamine activities. You temporarily remove overstimulation so that your brain can re-sensitize itself to natural rewards — things like focus, creativity, and genuine connection.

Let's break down how to do it effectively.

**Step 1: Identify Your High-Dopamine Triggers**

Before you detox, you must identify your specific triggers — the activities that consume your attention and offer cheap, quick dopamine hits.

Common triggers include:

- Social media (Instagram, TikTok, Twitter, YouTube)
- Streaming platforms (Netflix, Prime Video, etc.)
- Video games
- Junk food or sugar
- Shopping or online browsing
- Constant message checking
- News or gossip sites
- Excessive caffeine
- Pornography or sexual content

Spend one full day observing your habits. Keep a small notebook or use your journal to track:

- When do I reach for my phone without thinking?
- Which apps or sites consume most of my time?
- How do I feel before and after using them?

Awareness is half the battle. Once you identify your triggers, you can begin reclaiming control.

---

**Step 2: Choose Your Detox Type**

There are two main ways to do a dopamine detox:

**1. The Complete Detox (24–48 hours)**

For 1–2 days, eliminate all non-essential stimulation. This includes:

- No social media or internet browsing
- No TV or streaming
- No music (except calming instrumental or meditation)
- No junk food, sugar, alcohol, or caffeine
- No unnecessary phone use
- No multitasking

What you *can* do:

- Journal or meditate
- Go for walks in nature
- Read physical books
- Reflect on your goals and priorities
- Spend time in silence
- Practice gratitude
- Engage in creative hobbies like writing or drawing

At first, it will feel uncomfortable — you'll notice boredom, restlessness, and an almost physical urge to reach for your phone. That's your brain craving its fix. Resist the urge. Within 24 hours, you'll start feeling calmer and more grounded.

By the end of 48 hours, you'll likely notice something profound: stillness feels good again.

**2. The Sustainable Detox (Long-Term Reset)**

After your complete detox, transition into a sustainable, long-term routine that limits unnecessary dopamine triggers while promoting deep focus.

Here's how:

- Schedule social media time (e.g., 30 minutes in the evening)
- Keep your phone outside your bedroom
- Block distracting websites during work hours
- Practice "single-tasking" — doing one thing at a time
- Replace screen time with learning, reflection, or real conversation

The goal isn't to renounce pleasure — it's to **retrain your brain to enjoy the right kind of pleasure**.

---

**Step 3: Redesign Your Environment**

Your willpower is limited, but your environment is powerful. Make it easy to do what matters and hard to do what doesn't.

Here are practical strategies:

- **Out of sight, out of mind:** Keep your phone in another room during deep work. Disable unnecessary notifications.
- **Digital hygiene:** Uninstall non-essential apps from your home screen.
- **Create friction:** If you want to reduce social media use, log out after each session so logging in requires effort.
- **Make focus easy:** Keep your workspace clean, well-lit, and free of distractions.
- **Set up cues for good habits:** Keep a book on your desk. Leave your journal open. Place water nearby to encourage hydration.

When your environment supports your goals, discipline becomes effortless.

---

**Step 4: Embrace Boredom and Stillness**

In the modern world, boredom has become the enemy. We avoid it like a plague, filling every gap with scrolling or noise. But here's the secret: **boredom is the birthplace of creativity**.

When your brain is free from constant input, it begins to wander, imagine, and connect ideas. Some of history's greatest breakthroughs were born in boredom — Archimedes in his bath, Newton under a tree, Einstein while daydreaming.

Next time you feel bored, resist the urge to escape it. Sit with it. Observe your thoughts. Let your mind rest and reset. You might be surprised by the ideas that surface.

Practice "intentional boredom." Try spending ten minutes each day doing absolutely nothing — no phone, no book, no noise. Just breathe and observe. Over time, you'll develop comfort in stillness, a superpower in a hyperactive world.

---

**Step 5: Rebuild Focus Through Deep Work**

Once your brain begins to detox from overstimulation, you'll notice your attention span expanding again. This is the perfect time to reintroduce **deep work** — focused, distraction-free effort on something meaningful.

Cal Newport, author of *Deep Work,* defines it as "professional activities performed in a state of distraction-free concentration that push your cognitive capabilities to their limit."

Here's how to practice it:

1. **Time Block:** Schedule 90-minute deep work sessions where you focus on a single task — no notifications, no multitasking.
2. **Set Clear Goals:** Before you begin, know exactly what you want to accomplish.
3. **Create Rituals:** Work in the same space, at the same time daily.
4. **Take Purposeful Breaks:** After each deep session, rest — walk, stretch, or meditate.
5. **Track Progress:** Keep a log of how many hours you spend in deep work each week.

Deep work feels challenging at first, but soon it becomes deeply satisfying. It's where mastery is born — in the silence between distractions.

---

### Step 6: Reconnect with Natural Rewards

As your dopamine balance resets, you'll begin to rediscover joy in simple things:

- The warmth of morning sunlight
- A meaningful conversation
- The quiet satisfaction of completing a task
- The peace of a walk without your phone

These experiences release steady, sustainable dopamine — the kind that fuels contentment, not chaos.

You'll begin to notice that presence feels more fulfilling than pleasure, and focus feels better than distraction.

---

### The Link Between Dopamine and Discipline

Your ability to focus is directly tied to your ability to delay gratification. Every time you resist a quick dopamine hit — by not checking your phone, not giving in to procrastination — you strengthen your discipline muscle.

Over time, this builds what psychologists call **"attention capital"** — the capacity to direct your attention wherever you choose, for as long as you choose.

That's freedom. Because true freedom isn't doing whatever you want — it's having the power to focus on what truly matters.

---

### The Morning "No-Phone" Ritual

If you only change one thing after reading this chapter, let it be this: **start your mornings without your phone.**

When you check your phone first thing, you hand control of your attention to the world. You start your day reacting instead of creating.

Try this instead:

1. Don't touch your phone for the first 60 minutes after waking.
2. Use that hour to hydrate, move your body, meditate, read, or journal.
3. When you finally check messages, do so with intention — not compulsion.

This single habit can transform your productivity, peace, and self-mastery.

---

### Rediscovering the Joy of Focus

When was the last time you lost yourself so completely in something that time disappeared?

That's the state of **flow** — where your skills perfectly match your challenge, and you feel fully alive. It's the most productive and fulfilling state a human can experience.

Flow doesn't happen when you're multitasking or distracted. It happens when your mind is still, your attention is undivided, and your purpose is clear.

A dopamine detox helps you access that state more easily, because it removes the noise that scatters your energy.

As you train your brain to love focus again, you'll find that deep work and calm presence bring far more joy than any screen ever could.

---

## REFLECTION QUESTIONS

1. What are my top three high-dopamine distractions, and how do they affect my focus or mood?
2. When was the last time I experienced deep focus or flow, and what conditions made it possible?
3. What would I gain — mentally, emotionally, and spiritually — if I reduced digital distractions by 50% this week?

---

## AFFIRMATIONS FOR REPROGRAMMING

- My attention is precious, and I choose to invest it wisely.
- Focus is my new superpower; I direct it toward what truly matters.
- Stillness is not empty — it is full of creativity, clarity, and peace.

---

## PRACTICAL ACTION STEPS

1. **48-Hour Detox:** Schedule a weekend where you eliminate unnecessary technology. Spend time in silence, nature, and reflection.
2. **Digital Declutter:** Delete unused apps and turn off non-essential notifications.
3. **No-Phone Morning:** Commit to one hour every morning without screens.
4. **Deep Work Routine:** Schedule two distraction-free focus blocks daily (90 minutes each).

5. **Journal Prompt:** Each night, reflect: "Did I control my attention today, or did my distractions control me?"

# CHAPTER 4: THINK AND GROW RICH — THE FORMULA FOR SUCCESS

## PART 1: PRINCIPLES 1–7

### The Timeless Blueprint of Success

When Napoleon Hill first published *Think and Grow Rich* in 1937, he didn't just write a book — he revealed a *blueprint* for human achievement. His 13 principles weren't about getting rich in money alone; they were about **getting rich in life** — in confidence, purpose, relationships, and contribution.

Nearly a century later, his wisdom remains just as relevant. Technology has changed. The world has evolved. But the psychology of success — the way thoughts become things — has not.

In this chapter, we'll modernize Hill's classic 13 principles into a roadmap you can apply today. These are not abstract ideas — they are *laws of growth*. And when you apply them with belief, consistency, and courage, they can transform your life.

---

### 1. Desire — The Starting Point of All Achievement

Every success story begins with one thing: **burning desire**.

Desire is the spark that ignites the fire of action. Without it, no amount of talent, knowledge, or luck can move you forward.

Hill said, *"The starting point of all achievement is desire."* Desire is not mere wishing. Wishing says, "I'd like to have that." Desire says, "I will have that — no matter how long it takes or what it requires."

Look at every great innovator — Elon Musk risking his fortune to build SpaceX, Oprah Winfrey rising from poverty to global influence, or Thomas Edison failing a thousand times before success. What drove them was not luck — it was desire so powerful that failure couldn't extinguish it.

Desire creates energy. Energy fuels action. And action, sustained over time, creates success.

So ask yourself:

"What do I *really* want?"

Not what society tells you to want. Not what looks good on paper. What do you truly crave from your heart and soul?

Once you identify it, write it down. Describe it in detail. See it. Feel it. Touch it in your imagination until it becomes real.

**Desire gives birth to clarity — and clarity attracts opportunity.**

---

**2. Faith — Believing Before Seeing**

Desire alone is not enough. You must **believe** that what you desire is possible.

Faith is the invisible bridge between thought and reality. It is the ability to hold onto your vision even when circumstances contradict it.

Hill wrote, *"Whatever the mind can conceive and believe, it can achieve."*

That statement has built empires, launched careers, and healed lives.

Faith is not blind hope — it's *mental certainty*. It's the confident knowing that even if you can't see the path, the path exists.

Modern neuroscience backs this up: when you visualize success vividly and repeatedly, your brain's neural circuits fire as if the experience were already happening. Over time, those mental images reprogram your subconscious mind to seek and create that reality.

To strengthen your faith:

- Repeat positive affirmations daily (as you learned in Chapter 1).
- Visualize your desired outcome vividly.
- Surround yourself with people who believe in you.
- Take small steps that prove your belief true.

Faith grows through *evidence* — the evidence you create by acting despite doubt.

When you act in faith, you're telling the universe, "I trust that my vision is real — even before I can see it." And the universe always responds to faith in motion.

---

**3. Autosuggestion — Programming the Mind for Success**

Your subconscious mind is the most loyal servant you have. It accepts whatever you tell it repeatedly — especially when charged with emotion.

Autosuggestion is the deliberate use of words and imagery to influence your subconscious programming. Hill called it *"the medium through which you can voluntarily feed your subconscious mind with thoughts of your own choosing."*

Here's the truth: your life is a reflection of the thoughts you have impressed upon your subconscious. If you constantly feed it fear, it produces limitation. If you feed it confidence, it produces success.

The process of autosuggestion involves three key steps:

1. **Define your desire clearly.** Write a concise statement of what you want and by when.

2. **Repeat it daily — morning and night.** Speak it aloud with conviction, as if it's already true.

3. **Visualize the feeling of achievement.** Feel gratitude and excitement as if your goal were accomplished.

Example:

"I am now earning ₹25 lakh annually through meaningful work that inspires others, and I'm grateful for the impact I create."

When you repeat this daily, your subconscious begins to align your thoughts, emotions, and actions with that reality.

**Autosuggestion turns desire and faith into subconscious certainty — and certainty turns into results.**

---

**4. Specialized Knowledge — The Key to Leverage**

Knowledge is only potential power; **applied knowledge** is real power.

In the information age, we're surrounded by data — but success belongs to those who can turn that data into insight, and insight into action.

Hill observed that general knowledge — even college education — rarely creates wealth. It's **specialized knowledge**, organized and applied with purpose, that does.

Think of it this way: general knowledge fills your mind; specialized knowledge fills your bank account.

Every great achiever found a specific area of focus and mastered it. Jeff Bezos specialized in digital commerce logistics. Steve Jobs specialized in user-centered design. Serena Williams specialized in one craft — tennis — until she became a legend.

Ask yourself:

- What specific skill or expertise can I develop that solves real problems?
- How can I organize my learning to create value for others?

The modern world rewards depth, not breadth. Instead of trying to know everything, master something — then leverage it.

Combine specialized knowledge with creativity, and you'll always find opportunity.

---

**5. Imagination — The Workshop of the Mind**

Everything that exists — from airplanes to smartphones — began as an idea in someone's imagination.

Imagination is not a child's toy; it's the **workshop of the mind**. It's where all plans are shaped before they are transformed into reality.

Hill described two types of imagination:

- **Synthetic imagination:** rearranging old ideas into new combinations.
- **Creative imagination:** tapping into intuition or "Infinite Intelligence" for entirely new ideas.

In modern terms, creative imagination is flow — that state of effortless creation when ideas seem to download from a higher source.

To awaken your imagination, you must give yourself permission to dream boldly again. Adults often suppress imagination because they fear judgment or failure. But all innovation, all progress, all beauty begins with imagining something better.

Albert Einstein once said, *"Imagination is more important than knowledge."* He understood that while knowledge defines what exists, imagination defines what's possible.

Practical ways to reignite imagination:

- Spend 10 minutes a day visualizing your ideal future.
- Keep an "idea journal" — capture every creative spark.
- Expose yourself to new experiences — travel, read, converse deeply.
- Spend time in solitude; imagination needs silence to speak.

Remember: logic will take you from A to B. Imagination will take you anywhere.

---

**6. Organized Planning — Turning Dreams into Blueprints**

Desire and imagination are the seeds of success, but **planning** is the soil where they grow roots.

Hill wrote, *"No individual has ever achieved lasting success without plans that are definite, and based upon practical knowledge."*

Most people fail not because they lack dreams, but because they never create a clear, actionable plan to achieve them.

A plan turns wishful thinking into a step-by-step strategy.

To create your **Organized Plan**:

1. **Define your major goal** — clearly and specifically.
2. **Break it down** into smaller, measurable milestones.
3. **Set deadlines** — what gets scheduled gets done.

4. **Identify resources** — skills, mentors, finances, and networks you need.

5. **Take immediate action** — start with what you have.

Don't wait for perfect conditions — they never come. Your plan doesn't have to be flawless; it just has to be *in motion*. You can always adjust along the way.

Hill also emphasized collaboration: "No plan is sound unless it can be executed by a group of people working in harmony." This is why the **Mastermind principle** (coming later) is so powerful — you magnify your results through collective intelligence.

Example:
When Elon Musk set out to colonize Mars, he didn't just dream — he planned. He assembled experts, built prototypes, tested relentlessly, and adjusted strategies. The plan evolved, but the mission never changed.

That's how vision becomes victory.

---

**7. Decision — The Power of Commitment**

Successful people make decisions quickly and change them slowly. Unsuccessful people make decisions slowly and change them quickly.

Indecision is the silent killer of dreams. Every time you hesitate, doubt grows. Every time you act decisively, confidence grows.

Hill noted that procrastination is the opposite of decision. Fear of criticism, failure, or rejection keeps most people stuck in endless analysis.

The cure is **commitment** — the decision to act even when you don't have all the answers.

Look at Steve Jobs. When Apple was struggling, he made bold, fast decisions: simplify the product line, focus on design, trust intuition. Those decisions revived the company and redefined industries.

In your own life, decision-making is a muscle. The more you use it, the stronger it becomes.

Ask yourself:

- What decision have I been postponing?
- What's the cost of not deciding?
- What's one small action I can take right now to move forward?

Remember: indecision is still a decision — a decision to stay stuck.

The moment you commit, momentum begins. The universe rewards clarity.

# CHAPTER 4: THINK AND GROW RICH — THE FORMULA FOR SUCCESS

## PART 2: PRINCIPLES 8–13 + CONCLUSION

### 8. Persistence — The Iron Quality of Success

If desire is the seed of success, **persistence** is the water that nourishes it.
Every dream that ever became reality was sustained by someone who refused to quit.

Napoleon Hill said, *"Persistence is to the character of man what carbon is to steel."* Without persistence, the strongest desire fades into wishful thinking. With persistence, even impossible goals become inevitable.

Think of J.K. Rowling, who faced 12 publisher rejections before *Harry Potter* saw the light of day. Or Colonel Sanders, who was turned down more than a thousand times before one restaurant accepted his chicken recipe at age 65.

What kept them going? **Faith fused with persistence.**

Persistence isn't about blind stubbornness — it's about emotional endurance. It's choosing to keep showing up even when results are invisible. Every rejection is feedback, every setback a lesson, every delay a test of your commitment.

Here's a truth few realize: the universe often delays success not to punish you, but to prepare you — to strengthen your character for the greatness you've asked for.

To build persistence:

- **Anchor your purpose:** Remind yourself *why* you started.
- **Celebrate progress:** Reward small wins; they fuel momentum.

- **Expect resistance:** Every worthwhile goal will test your patience.
- **Replace quitting with resting:** Pause, recover, but never retreat.

Remember — the race doesn't always go to the fastest, but to the one who refuses to stop running.

---

**9. The Mastermind — The Power of Collective Energy**

No one succeeds alone.

Hill's **Mastermind principle** states: "When two or more minds come together in harmony, a third invisible mind — a greater power — is created."

That's not just philosophy — it's physics. When people align their intentions and energy, synergy emerges. One person's strength amplifies another's vision. Ideas expand. Momentum multiplies.

Look at history's great partnerships:

- **Wright brothers** — innovation through collaboration.
- **Steve Jobs and Steve Wozniak** — creativity meets engineering.
- **Bill Gates and Paul Allen, Sergey Brin and Larry Page** — the pattern repeats.

In business, leadership, or personal growth, your environment shapes your elevation. The people you surround yourself with either pull you down or push you higher.

To build your own Mastermind:

1. **Find your tribe:** Surround yourself with growth-oriented individuals who challenge you.

2. **Meet consistently:** Once a week or month, share goals, challenges, and wins.

3. **Encourage accountability:** Each person commits to action steps.

4. **Collaborate energetically:** Offer ideas freely, without ego.

A true Mastermind isn't about hierarchy — it's about harmony. It's about fusing minds in pursuit of a shared vision.

When you align with others on the same frequency of ambition and faith, you plug into exponential power.

---

**10. The Subconscious Mind — The Gateway to Infinite Intelligence**

You learned earlier that the subconscious is your silent partner — but here, Hill deepens that truth.

Your **subconscious mind** connects you directly to the infinite intelligence of the universe. It's the bridge between your conscious desires and the creative force that manifests them.

Whatever thoughts you feed it — faith or fear, success or failure — it magnifies and reflects in your experience.

Hill said, *"The subconscious mind works day and night, through methods of its own, to translate desire into its physical equivalent."*

This is where belief meets manifestation.

Modern neuroscience agrees. Repeated thoughts form neural pathways; over time, they shape your automatic behavior, perception, and opportunities.

To program your subconscious for success:

- Use **affirmations** that evoke strong emotion.
- **Visualize** your desired outcome as already real.
- Maintain **gratitude** — it signals abundance to your mind.
- Guard your mind vigilantly — avoid negative input and gossip.

Think of your subconscious as fertile soil. Whatever seeds you plant — thoughts, emotions, or words — will grow. Choose them consciously.

When your subconscious is trained to expect success, the world must conform.

---

### 11. The Brain — Your Broadcasting and Receiving Station

Your brain is not just a biological organ — it's an **energy transmitter**. Hill believed that your brain, when charged with emotion and purpose, emits vibrations that attract corresponding frequencies.

In modern language, this is resonance — the idea that energy attracts like energy.

Have you ever thought about someone intensely, and they called you? Or fixated on a goal, and then saw opportunities appear everywhere? That's not coincidence — it's alignment.

When your thoughts, emotions, and actions vibrate in harmony with your goals, your brain becomes a magnet for circumstances that match your mental frequency.

Practically speaking:

- **Focus daily** on what you *want*, not what you *fear*.
- **Feed your brain** with inspiration, not noise.

- **Protect your attention** — your brain rewires based on what you repeatedly focus on.

Your brain doesn't distinguish between imagination and reality — it simply responds to the dominant vibration you project.

When you maintain a high mental frequency — of gratitude, love, and confidence — you draw people, opportunities, and ideas of the same vibration.

Your brain is your most advanced technology. Use it consciously, and it will broadcast miracles.

### 12. The Sixth Sense — The Door to Intuition

Hill described the sixth sense as the "Temple of Wisdom." It's the channel through which ideas, insights, and solutions flow from Infinite Intelligence to your conscious mind.

In today's terms, we call it **intuition** — that quiet inner knowing that guides you even when logic can't explain it.

Have you ever had a hunch that turned out to be right? Or felt compelled to make a choice that didn't make sense at the time, but later proved perfect? That's your sixth sense speaking.

Intuition doesn't shout — it whispers. To hear it, you must quiet the noise.

You strengthen intuition by:

- **Meditating** daily to clear mental clutter.
- **Trusting small nudges** — each time you follow intuition, it grows stronger.
- **Asking questions** before sleep or reflection — your subconscious and intuition will answer.

- **Acting quickly** when insight strikes — hesitation weakens intuitive signals.

Albert Einstein credited intuition for his breakthroughs, saying, *"The intuitive mind is a sacred gift, and the rational mind is a faithful servant."*

Your goal is balance — to use logic for planning, and intuition for direction.

When your mind is calm, your sixth sense opens. And when it opens, you'll realize you're never truly alone — guidance is always within reach.

---

### 13. The Mystery of Sex Transmutation — Channeling Creative Energy

Hill's final principle often raises eyebrows — **Sex Transmutation.** But it's one of his most profound insights.

He discovered that sexual energy, when redirected toward creative or productive outlets, becomes one of the most powerful forces for success.

Sex energy is life energy — the pure creative force that drives passion, ambition, and vitality. Most people dissipate it through indulgence or distraction. The masters, however, **transmute** it — they redirect it toward innovation, art, leadership, and achievement.

When you focus that same intensity and passion into your goals, your mind and body synchronize in peak creativity.

Practical ways to apply this:

- Channel passion into meaningful work or purpose.
- Exercise regularly to convert physical energy into mental clarity.

- Avoid overindulgence in any sensory pleasure; it drains willpower.
- Use emotional energy — love, inspiration, desire — as creative fuel.

Many of history's most influential leaders were intensely passionate people — not just romantically, but in their devotion to their craft.

Passion is divine energy. When you learn to harness it, your life becomes electrified with purpose.

---

**The Ultimate Synthesis — How the 13 Principles Interconnect**

Each of these principles works like a gear in the same machine.

- **Desire** gives you direction.
- **Faith** gives you confidence.
- **Autosuggestion** programs your subconscious.
- **Specialized Knowledge** sharpens your tools.
- **Imagination** designs the vision.
- **Organized Planning** builds the roadmap.
- **Decision** turns thought into action.
- **Persistence** sustains effort.
- **The Mastermind** amplifies power.
- **The Subconscious Mind** connects to infinite intelligence.
- **The Brain** broadcasts and attracts.

- **The Sixth Sense** guides intuition.
- **Sex Transmutation** fuels creativity and drive.

When aligned, they create a **complete success system** — mental, emotional, and spiritual harmony directed toward one clear purpose.

The greatest secret of *Think and Grow Rich* is not merely to "think" — but to *become* the person whose thinking naturally creates success.

You don't chase wealth, health, or fulfillment; you *become* the kind of person who attracts them.

---

**Modern-Day Example: The Power of Integration**

Take Elon Musk. Whether you agree with him or not, he's a living embodiment of Hill's principles:

- **Desire:** Colonizing Mars and revolutionizing transport.
- **Faith:** Persisting through bankruptcy threats and ridicule.
- **Autosuggestion:** Reiterating his mission daily.
- **Specialized Knowledge:** Engineering, physics, and leadership.
- **Imagination:** Visualizing electric cars and space travel as normal.
- **Organized Planning:** Recruiting top talent and building infrastructure.
- **Decision:** Acting swiftly and fearlessly.
- **Persistence:** Refusing to give up after multiple failures.

- **Mastermind:** Aligning with brilliant minds across industries.
- **Subconscious Mind:** Visualizing future possibilities vividly.
- **Brain:** Broadcasting purpose and attracting investors.
- **Sixth Sense:** Trusting instinct over convention.
- **Sex Transmutation:** Channeling massive energy into creation.

His journey proves that when all principles align, reality bends to purpose.

---

**Reflection Questions**

1. Which of the 13 principles do I naturally practice well, and which need development?
2. What is one area in my life where I've given up too soon — and how can I apply persistence now?
3. Who could be part of my "Mastermind group," and how can I begin forming it this month?
4. What intuitive nudges or inner callings have I been ignoring lately?

---

**Affirmations for Reprogramming**

- I am the architect of my destiny; my thoughts shape my reality.
- My desire is backed by unshakable faith and relentless action.
- I attract the right people, ideas, and opportunities in perfect timing.
- My imagination is unlimited; I turn dreams into tangible results.
- I persist until success is inevitable.

---

**Practical Action Steps**

1. **Create a Desire Statement:** Write your main life goal clearly, including timeline, emotional reason, and plan. Read it aloud twice daily.
2. **Mastermind Formation:** Identify 3–5 people aligned with your vision. Schedule monthly growth meetings.

3. **Faith Practice:** Begin every morning with visualization and gratitude to train belief.
4. **Persistence Challenge:** Choose one goal you've delayed and commit to consistent daily progress for 30 days.
5. **Intuition Journal:** Record intuitive insights and decisions you acted upon. Review weekly to build trust in your inner guidance.

---

**Closing Thoughts: From Thinking to Becoming**

You don't "think and grow rich" by daydreaming — you grow rich by **thinking correctly**, **feeling deeply**, and **acting consistently.**

Success is never a single event; it's a daily alignment of your inner world with your outer actions.

The formula Hill uncovered nearly a century ago still holds true because it speaks to timeless laws — the laws of thought, emotion, energy, and faith.

When you master these, you don't just attract success — you *embody* it. You become the Unstoppable You

# CHAPTER 5: THE POWER OF SELF-DISCIPLINE AND HABITS

**The Bridge Between Dreams and Reality**

Everyone has dreams. Only a few turn them into reality.

What separates those few from the rest isn't luck, talent, or resources — it's **self-discipline**.

Self-discipline is the invisible bridge between where you are and where you want to be. It's what carries you across when motivation fades and obstacles appear.

In every field — business, art, science, athletics — the top performers share one trait: they *do the work even when they don't feel like it.*

Motivation gets you started. Discipline keeps you going.

Think about it:

- Motivation is emotional. It comes and goes.
- Discipline is habitual. It stays even when emotions don't.

The truth is, no one feels inspired every day. But disciplined people act anyway. They've trained their minds and habits to work *for* them, not *against* them.

Self-discipline isn't punishment. It's **self-respect** — a declaration that your long-term goals are more important than your short-term impulses.

**The Psychology of Discipline: Mastering the Inner Battle**

At its core, discipline is an internal dialogue — a conversation between two selves:

- The **present self** that seeks comfort, and

- The **future self** that seeks greatness.

Every time you choose discipline, you honor your future self. Every time you give in to distraction, you betray it.

Psychologists call this **delayed gratification** — the ability to resist an immediate reward for a greater one later. The famous **Stanford marshmallow experiment** proved that children who delayed eating one marshmallow to receive two later grew up to have better health, finances, and relationships.

That's the power of restraint.

You can apply this principle to anything:

- Resisting the urge to scroll when you should study.
- Saying no to extra spending to save for your goals.
- Sticking to your workout when you'd rather sleep.

Each act of discipline strengthens your willpower muscle.

**The Science Behind Willpower**

Willpower is not infinite; it's like a battery. Throughout the day, decisions drain it — what to wear, what to eat, what to say. That's why successful people minimize trivial choices to preserve energy for what matters.

Steve Jobs famously wore the same black turtleneck every day to avoid "decision fatigue." Barack Obama and Mark Zuckerberg did the same.

They understood that discipline thrives when decisions are **automated**— when good habits replace constant deliberation.

That's where habits come in.

---

**Habits: The Automation of Excellence**

Aristotle said, *"We are what we repeatedly do. Excellence, then, is not an act, but a habit."*

Habits are the foundation of success because they make good behavior effortless. Once something becomes automatic, you no longer rely on motivation or willpower to do it.

Every habit follows a simple neurological loop, as described by Charles Duhigg in *The Power of Habit*:

**Cue → Routine → Reward**

- **Cue**: The trigger that starts the behavior (time, place, emotion, event).
- **Routine**: The behavior itself.
- **Reward**: The satisfaction or relief that reinforces the behavior.

To change any habit, you must identify and modify this loop.

Let's say you want to stop procrastinating.

- Cue: You sit down at your desk and feel overwhelmed.
- Routine: You grab your phone to escape discomfort.
- Reward: Temporary relief from anxiety.

To change it, keep the cue and reward but alter the routine:

- New routine: Take one small step on your task instead of checking your phone.
  Over time, your brain learns that *progress* provides the same relief — and a deeper satisfaction.

Small shifts lead to massive transformation.

### Keystone Habits: The Domino Effect of Change

Not all habits are equal. Some habits — called **keystone habits** — create positive ripple effects across your life.

Examples of keystone habits include:

- **Exercise:** Improves energy, confidence, mood, and focus.
- **Daily journaling:** Clarifies thought, reduces stress, boosts creativity.
- **Waking up early:** Creates time for reflection and goal setting.
- **Gratitude:** Trains your mind to see opportunities instead of problems.

Start with one keystone habit. As it strengthens, others will naturally follow.

Exercise leads to healthier eating. Journaling leads to better decision-making. Gratitude leads to patience and optimism.

The right habit triggers a chain reaction of growth.

---

### Building Discipline Through Environment Design

People often think they lack discipline when they really lack **environmental support.**

You don't rise to the level of your goals — you fall to the level of your systems.

If your environment constantly tempts you toward distraction, no amount of willpower will save you. But if your environment makes the right behavior easy, discipline becomes automatic.

**Simplify Your Surroundings**

1. **Remove temptation:** Keep your phone in another room during focus time.

2. **Visual cues:** Keep a water bottle on your desk, running shoes near the door, a book beside your bed.

3. **Create friction for bad habits:** If you overuse social media, log out after every session or delete the app from your home screen.

4. **Design a sacred workspace:** Keep your work area tidy, well-lit, and free from clutter.

Your environment should constantly whisper your goals back to you.

**Habit Stacking**

A powerful method from James Clear's *Atomic Habits* is **habit stacking**— linking a new behavior to an existing one.

- "After I brush my teeth, I'll meditate for two minutes."
- "After I pour my morning coffee, I'll review my goals."

This technique uses your brain's existing patterns to install new ones.

---

**Discipline as Emotional Intelligence**

Self-discipline isn't just about control — it's about **emotional mastery**.

The disciplined person doesn't suppress emotions; they manage them. They don't react impulsively to stress, anger, or boredom. Instead, they respond intentionally.

When you feel tempted to procrastinate or quit, pause and ask:

"What emotion am I trying to escape right now?"

Often, we avoid tasks not because they're hard, but because they make us uncomfortable. Discipline means facing discomfort directly and transforming it into growth.

That's how you develop **emotional resilience** — the ability to stay steady when life gets turbulent.

---

**The Power of Routine and Consistency**

Success isn't built in bursts of greatness; it's built in daily repetition.

Your routines shape your destiny. The small, consistent actions you take every day — reading for 20 minutes, saving a portion of income, practicing gratitude — compound over time.

Compounding is the hidden multiplier of success. Just as money grows through interest, habits grow through consistency.

The key is not intensity but **consistency**.
It's better to work out for 20 minutes every day than 2 hours once a week.
Better to read 10 pages daily than binge one book a month.

Consistency creates rhythm. Rhythm builds momentum. Momentum becomes identity.

---

**Identity-Based Habits: Becoming, Not Just Doing**

The most powerful way to change behavior is not by focusing on what you want to achieve, but on **who you want to become.**

Instead of saying, "I want to write a book," say, "I am a writer."
Instead of, "I want to exercise more," say, "I am an athlete."
Instead of, "I want to be disciplined," say, "I am a disciplined person."

Identity shapes action. When you align your habits with your identity, discipline becomes natural.

Every small win reinforces that identity. Each time you act in alignment with your ideal self, you strengthen that belief.

Change is not about forcing a new behavior — it's about *remembering who you truly are.*

---

**Modern Examples of Discipline in Action**

**1. Serena Williams — Discipline as Mastery**

Serena didn't become a tennis legend by talent alone. She trained every morning, even after victories. She practiced her serve until it became reflex. Her secret wasn't motivation — it was ritual.

She once said, *"I really think a champion is defined not by their wins but by how they can recover when they fall."* That's discipline — the will to show up no matter what.

**2. Elon Musk — Relentless Consistency**

At the height of SpaceX failures, Musk split his time between Tesla and SpaceX, working 100-hour weeks. His schedule was divided into 5-minute blocks.

He didn't rely on feelings. He relied on focus and structure.

His philosophy: "If something is important enough, you do it even if the odds are not in your favor."

**3. Marie Curie — Focused Obsession**

Marie Curie spent years isolating radium through painstaking experiments, often working 18-hour days. Her focus changed science forever.

Discipline gave her what talent alone could not — results.

These stories prove one thing: Discipline is not about perfection. It's about persistence.

---

**Overcoming Resistance: The War Within**

You'll face resistance — the invisible force that tries to stop you from doing meaningful work.

Steven Pressfield calls it *"The Resistance."* It's procrastination, self-doubt, and distraction disguised as comfort.

You defeat resistance not by fighting it, but by showing up anyway. Action dissolves fear.

The hardest part is starting. Once you begin, momentum takes over.

Next time you feel resistance, count down from five and move — *5, 4, 3, 2, 1 — go.*
This small trick, popularized by Mel Robbins, interrupts hesitation and activates action.

Courage isn't the absence of fear; it's the decision to move forward despite it.

---

**Morning Mastery: Setting the Tone for the Day**

Your morning determines your mindset.

When you start your day with intention instead of reaction, you set yourself up for success.

A powerful morning routine doesn't need to be long — just consistent.

Here's a simple structure (The "MAGIC Hour"):

1. **M — Movement:** 10–15 minutes of physical activity.
2. **A — Affirmation:** Revisit goals and speak your intentions.
3. **G — Gratitude:** Write three things you're thankful for.
4. **I — Inspiration:** Read or listen to something uplifting.
5. **C — Creation:** Spend time on one meaningful task before checking your phone.

Start with 30–60 minutes. Over time, this routine reprograms your brain for productivity, clarity, and calm.

---

**Evening Excellence: The Reflection Ritual**

Just as the morning sets your tone, your evening seals your growth.

Before bed, spend 10 minutes reflecting:

- What went well today?
- What could I improve tomorrow?
- Did I live in alignment with my values?

Write down your key lessons and intentions for tomorrow. Then disconnect from devices at least 30 minutes before sleep.

This nightly closure sends a clear signal to your subconscious: "The day is complete. I am at peace."

Discipline isn't only about doing — it's also about knowing when to rest.

---

**Reflection Questions**

1. In what areas of my life do I most struggle with discipline, and why?
2. What keystone habit could I install this month to elevate every area of my life?
3. How does my environment support — or sabotage — my goals?
4. What emotion usually drives my procrastination, and how can I respond differently next time?

---

**Affirmations for Reprogramming**

- I am a disciplined, focused, and purpose-driven individual.
- My habits align with my highest self and long-term vision.
- I do what needs to be done, even when I don't feel like it.
- Consistency is my superpower; every small step compounds toward greatness.

---

**Practical Action Steps**

1. **Choose one keystone habit** to focus on for 30 days (exercise, journaling, meditation, or reading).
2. **Design your environment** to make discipline easy — remove distractions and add visual cues.
3. **Create a morning and evening routine** using the MAGIC structure.
4. **Track your habits daily** in a journal or app.

5. **Celebrate small wins** — reward consistency, not perfection.

---

**Closing Thoughts: Discipline is Freedom**

At first, discipline feels restrictive. But soon, you realize — it's the opposite.

Discipline is freedom. Freedom from chaos. Freedom from guilt. Freedom from regret.

When your habits align with your goals, life becomes simpler. You no longer wrestle with indecision or guilt — you act. You trust yourself.

Every time you keep a promise to yourself, you build integrity. And integrity builds confidence.

Discipline is the highest form of self-love — because it honors your future over your impulse.

# CHAPTER 6: THE POWER OF EMOTIONAL INTELLIGENCE

## PART 1: PERSONAL EMOTIONAL MASTERY

### The Hidden Force Behind Every Success

Have you ever wondered why some people with average intelligence rise to extraordinary success, while others with high IQs struggle to reach their potential?

The answer lies not in intellect — but in **emotional intelligence**.

Emotional Intelligence (EQ) is the ability to understand and manage emotions — both your own and those of others. It's the key that unlocks resilience, focus, and authentic confidence.

Harvard research shows that **EQ accounts for nearly 90% of what separates high performers from average ones**. In leadership roles, it matters even more than technical skill.

You can have all the knowledge in the world, but if you can't regulate your emotions under pressure, communicate calmly, and stay centered through chaos, your potential remains unrealized.

Emotional intelligence is the art of mastering your inner world so you can thrive in the outer one.

---

### Self-Awareness: The First Step to Mastery

All transformation begins with awareness.

You can't change what you don't recognize.

Self-awareness is the foundation of emotional mastery — the ability to observe your thoughts, feelings, and triggers without being consumed by them.

Ask yourself:

- What emotions do I feel most often in a typical week?
- What patterns keep repeating in my reactions?
- How do my moods influence my decisions and energy?

Most people live on autopilot, reacting to emotions instead of responding with intention. But awareness creates a pause — and in that pause lies your power.

When you become aware of your emotions, you step out of identification with them. You're no longer *angry* — you're *observing anger*. You're no longer *anxious* — you're *aware of anxiety*.

That shift transforms everything.

Eckhart Tolle calls this *"watching the thinker."* It's the art of witnessing your emotions like clouds passing through the sky. They're not permanent. They're not who you are.

You are the sky — vast, steady, unchanging.

---

**Emotional Triggers: Turning Reaction into Response**

Your triggers are your teachers.

A "trigger" is an emotional reaction disproportionate to the situation. It's the past replaying in the present.

Maybe criticism makes you defensive because you once felt unheard. Maybe rejection feels unbearable because it echoes an old wound.

Each trigger points to an area that needs healing.

Instead of suppressing or judging it, **get curious**.
Ask:

"What story is this emotion trying to tell me?"

That curiosity transforms pain into power.

The next time someone triggers you, pause and breathe. Don't respond immediately. Instead, step back mentally:

1. Name the emotion: "I'm feeling angry."
2. Identify the trigger: "I felt dismissed."
3. Ask what it's showing you: "I want to feel respected."
4. Choose your response consciously.

This simple process breaks the cycle of reactivity and replaces it with awareness.

---

**Emotional Regulation: The Art of Inner Balance**

Emotional regulation doesn't mean suppressing your feelings — it means managing them skillfully.

Your emotions are data, not directives. They're messages, not masters.

When you feel stress, fear, or frustration, your brain releases cortisol and adrenaline — fight-or-flight chemicals. This reaction was useful for ancient survival, but in modern life, it often gets triggered by emails, deadlines, or social tension.

The goal isn't to eliminate emotion but to restore balance quickly.

Here are powerful ways to regulate emotions in the moment:

**1. The Power of the Pause**

Take three deep breaths. This interrupts the body's stress response and activates the parasympathetic nervous system — your "calm and connect" mode.

**2. Label the Emotion**

Research shows that simply naming what you feel ("I'm anxious," "I'm disappointed") reduces its intensity.

**3. Shift Physiology**

Move your body — walk, stretch, or stand tall. Physical movement shifts chemistry faster than thought alone.

**4. Reframe the Meaning**

Ask, "What else could this mean?" Reinterpret situations from a higher perspective.

For example:
Instead of "They're ignoring me," think "They might be busy — I'll check in later."
Instead of "I failed," think "I'm learning what doesn't work."

Reframing changes suffering into strength.

---

**The Power of Acceptance**

One of the hardest truths to accept is that **resisting emotions strengthens them**.

When you fight anger, it grows. When you resist fear, it lingers. When you judge sadness, it deepens.

Acceptance isn't weakness — it's wisdom.

To accept means to allow the emotion to exist without letting it define you. It's saying, "This feeling is here, and that's okay."

Acceptance softens the resistance and allows healing.

You can't heal what you hate — but you can transform what you accept.

This is what mindfulness really means: being present with what *is*, without labeling it as good or bad.

Try this short **"Feel It to Heal It"** exercise:

1. Close your eyes.
2. Bring attention to your body and notice where the emotion lives (chest, stomach, shoulders).
3. Breathe into that area gently, without trying to change it.
4. Say inwardly, "It's okay for me to feel this."
5. After a minute or two, observe how the emotion begins to dissolve naturally.

Every emotion wants acknowledgment, not avoidance.

---

**The Three Lies of Emotion**

Most people suffer not because of emotions themselves, but because they believe these three lies:

1. **"My emotions define me."**
   False. Emotions are temporary states — not your identity.
2. **"If I feel it, it must be true."**
   False. Emotions reflect perception, not objective reality. You can feel rejected even when you're valued.
3. **"I can't control my emotions."**
   False. You can't control what arises, but you can always control your response.

The moment you realize these truths, you reclaim your power.

---

### Emotional Resilience: Bouncing Forward, Not Back

Resilience isn't about avoiding breakdowns — it's about how quickly you recover from them.

Emotionally intelligent people don't stay down long. They process pain, extract lessons, and rise stronger.

When life challenges you — a failed project, a betrayal, a loss — your response determines your future. You can either break down or break through.

Resilient people share three key traits:

- **Perspective:** They see setbacks as temporary, not personal.
- **Purpose:** They find meaning in adversity.
- **Progress:** They focus on small wins that rebuild confidence.

As psychologist Viktor Frankl wrote in *Man's Search for Meaning*:

"When we are no longer able to change a situation, we are challenged to change ourselves."

Resilience is the art of self-renewal.

---

### The Energy of Emotion

Emotion = Energy in Motion.

Each emotion carries a vibration that affects your state. Gratitude and love uplift. Fear and resentment constrict.

The key is not to deny "negative" emotions but to **transmute** them — to move energy through action.

If you're angry — channel it into physical movement or creative work.
If you're sad — write, paint, or talk it out.
If you're anxious — move your breath deeper into your belly and focus on what's within control.

Emotional mastery isn't about feeling happy all the time — it's about staying steady no matter what you feel.

---

**Reclaiming Emotional Power**

When you stop being at the mercy of your emotions, you reclaim your life.

You no longer say, "I'm stressed because of them," or "They made me angry." You say, "I choose how to respond."

That shift — from reaction to responsibility — is the essence of empowerment.

The more emotionally aware you become, the more influence you have— not only over your own life but over others who look to you for guidance.

Before we move to the relational and leadership side of EQ in Part 2, let's integrate what we've covered with some self-reflective work.

---

**Reflection Questions**

1. What emotions dominate my daily life, and what might they be teaching me?
2. How do I typically respond when I feel triggered or stressed?
3. Which recurring emotional pattern am I ready to transform?
4. How can I practice mindfulness or emotional regulation in my daily routine?

---

**Affirmations for Emotional Mastery**

- I am aware of my emotions, but they do not control me.
- Every emotion is a messenger guiding me toward growth.
- I remain calm, centered, and confident in all situations.
- I honor what I feel, learn from it, and let it go with ease.

---

**Practical Action Steps**

1. **Daily Check-In:** Pause three times a day to ask, "What am I feeling right now, and why?"
2. **Breath Reset:** Use deep breathing whenever stress arises — inhale calm, exhale tension.
3. **Emotional Journal:** Spend 10 minutes each evening naming your emotions and how you responded.
4. **Trigger Awareness:** Identify one recurring emotional trigger and consciously apply a new response pattern this week.

# CHAPTER 6: THE POWER OF EMOTIONAL INTELLIGENCE

## PART 2: RELATIONAL & LEADERSHIP INTELLIGENCE

### The True Measure of Leadership

John C. Maxwell once said, *"Leadership is influence — nothing more, nothing less."*

But what determines the depth of your influence?
It's not your title, your intellect, or your technical skill. It's your **emotional intelligence** — the way you make others *feel* when they're around you.

People don't follow the smartest person in the room. They follow the one who listens, understands, and inspires.

This is the essence of **Relational and Leadership Intelligence** — the ability to sense, connect, and guide human emotions in a way that brings out the best in people.

Whether you're leading a company, a classroom, a team, or a family, your emotional intelligence defines your impact.

---

### 1. The Foundation: Empathy

Empathy is not weakness — it's a superpower.

To be empathetic is to *feel with* another person — to step into their shoes and understand their perspective without judgment.

In today's world of noise, speed, and digital disconnection, empathy is rare — and that makes it powerful.

Empathy transforms leadership from command to connection. It allows you to influence hearts, not just direct actions.

There are three levels of empathy:

1. **Cognitive Empathy** — Understanding someone's perspective intellectually.

"I see where you're coming from."

2. **Emotional Empathy** — Feeling what the other person feels.

"I can sense your frustration and pain."

3. **Compassionate Empathy** — Understanding, feeling, *and* taking helpful action.

"I know you're struggling — let's find a solution together."

Great leaders operate at the third level. They don't just sympathize; they mobilize support and trust.

When you truly listen — without agenda, without waiting to speak — people feel seen, valued, and understood. That's when they open up and give their best.

---

**2. The Art of Active Listening**

Listening is the most underrated leadership skill — and the rarest form of respect.

Most people listen to reply, not to understand. True listening is an act of presence.

Here's how to practice **Active Listening**:

1. **Be Fully Present:** Put away devices. Make eye contact. Give undivided attention.

2. **Listen for Emotion, Not Just Words:** What are they *really* feeling beneath the surface?

3. **Reflect Back:** Paraphrase their message — "So you're saying you felt overlooked in that meeting?"

4. **Pause Before Responding:** Silence shows respect and allows depth to emerge.

Active listening builds trust faster than any motivational speech ever could.

When people feel heard, they don't need convincing — they align naturally.

---

**3. Emotional Contagion: The Hidden Influence**

Emotions are contagious. Neuroscientists call this the **mirror neuron effect** — your brain subconsciously imitates the emotional state of people around you.

That means your mood as a leader sets the tone for everyone you influence.

If you're calm, confident, and positive, your team absorbs that stability. If you're anxious, irritable, or inconsistent, they mirror that too.

Energy is leadership.

This is why **self-regulation** — the ability to stay grounded under pres sure— is a critical leadership skill.

When chaos strikes, people don't look for instructions; they look for emotional cues. They look for *you*.

You don't have to be emotionless. You just have to be *emotionally centered.*

Practice this in stressful moments:

- Breathe slowly to steady your nervous system.
- Speak slowly and clearly — speed signals anxiety.
- Focus on solutions, not blame.
- Model calm even when you feel the storm.

Leadership isn't about having all the answers. It's about being the calm in the room when everyone else loses theirs.

---

**4. Building Emotional Trust**

Trust is the currency of leadership — and it's built emotionally, not logically.

You can't demand trust; you earn it through consistency, authenticity, and empathy.

People trust you when they feel safe with you — when they believe you have their back, not just their performance metrics.

Here's how to build **emotional trust**:

1. **Be Transparent:** Share information honestly, even when it's hard.
2. **Keep Promises:** Do what you say, every time.
3. **Admit Mistakes:** Vulnerability builds connection.
4. **Show Appreciation:** Recognize effort, not just results.

Leaders who show humility inspire loyalty. When you admit, "I was wrong," you don't lose authority — you gain authenticity.

Remember: people may forget what you said, but they'll never forget how you made them feel.

---

**5. Conflict Management with Emotional Intelligence**

Conflict is inevitable wherever humans interact. But emotionally intelligent leaders use conflict as a bridge, not a battlefield.

The goal isn't to win arguments — it's to find understanding.

Here's the **EQ approach to conflict resolution**:

1. **Pause Before Reacting:** Anger narrows perspective. Take a breath.
2. **Seek to Understand First:** Ask, "Can you help me understand your point of view?"
3. **Focus on Behavior, Not Personality:** Say, "When deadlines are missed..." instead of "You're irresponsible."
4. **Use "I" Statements:** Express your perspective without blame—"I feel concerned when communication breaks down."
5. **Find Common Ground:** Shift the focus from "me vs. you" to "us vs. the problem."

Remember: conflict is energy. Redirect it toward collaboration.

A team that avoids conflict stagnates. A team that manages it intelligently grows.

---

**6. Leading with Emotional Awareness**

Emotionally aware leaders understand that every person is driven by an inner world of hopes, fears, and values.

They don't lead by command — they lead by *connection.*

Daniel Goleman, who popularized EQ, found that the best leaders exhibit five emotional competencies:

1. **Self-Awareness** — Knowing one's emotions and their impact.
2. **Self-Regulation** — Staying composed and adaptable.
3. **Motivation** — Acting from inner purpose rather than external rewards.
4. **Empathy** — Understanding others' emotions.
5. **Social Skills** — Building relationships and influence.

These are not soft skills — they are *super skills.*

They determine whether a leader inspires voluntary effort or enforces compliance.

For example, when Satya Nadella took over as Microsoft CEO, he didn't just change strategy — he changed culture. He replaced a "know-it-all" mindset with a "learn-it-all" mindset, built on empathy and collaboration.

The result? Microsoft's value tripled within five years.

That's the power of emotionally intelligent leadership.

---

**7. Communication with Compassion and Clarity**

Great communication is not about speaking louder — it's about connecting deeper.

Emotionally intelligent communication blends **compassion** with **clarity**:

- Compassion ensures people feel valued.

- Clarity ensures they understand the message.

To master this balance, follow the **3 Cs of Emotional Communication**:

1. **Calm:** Deliver your message in a composed tone, even under stress.
2. **Curiosity:** Ask open-ended questions — “How do you see this?”
3. **Care:** Show genuine concern for how your words affect others.

Before every important conversation, ask yourself:

“What emotion do I want to leave them with?”

If your words uplift, inspire, or reassure — you’ve led well.

---

**8. Emotional Intelligence in Teams**

Teams are emotional ecosystems. The collective mood shapes creativity, collaboration, and performance.

As a leader, your job is to **regulate the emotional climate** of your team.

**How to Create Emotionally Intelligent Teams:**

1. **Model openness:** Share your challenges honestly — it encourages authenticity.
2. **Encourage feedback:** Create a culture where speaking up feels safe.
3. **Recognize effort publicly:** Appreciation fuels motivation.
4. **Celebrate small wins:** Momentum grows through recognition.
5. **Resolve tension early:** Unspoken frustration poisons morale.

Google's "Project Aristotle" found that the most successful teams weren't the smartest — they were the most **psychologically safe**. Members felt accepted, respected, and free to express themselves without fear.

When people feel safe, they innovate. When they feel threatened, they hide.

Emotional safety breeds collective brilliance.

---

**9. Leading Through Change and Uncertainty**

In times of change — layoffs, reorganization, crisis — emotions run high.

Facts alone won't calm fear. People don't need more data; they need emotional grounding.

An emotionally intelligent leader acknowledges feelings before addressing strategy.

Try this sequence when leading through uncertainty:

1. **Acknowledge Emotion:** "I understand this situation feels unsettling."
2. **Validate Experience:** "It's okay to feel anxious — we're human."
3. **Provide Direction:** "Here's what we know, and here's our next step."
4. **Reinforce Confidence:** "We've overcome challenges before, and we'll do it again."

Leadership during crisis isn't about having perfect answers — it's about creating emotional stability amid uncertainty.

When you lead with empathy and transparency, fear transforms into trust.

**10. The Energy of Service and Influence**

At the highest level, emotional intelligence evolves into **servant leadership** — leading not from ego, but from purpose.

The emotionally intelligent leader doesn't say, "Follow me." They say, "Let's go together."

They see their role not as commanding others, but as empowering them.

As Simon Sinek teaches in *Leaders Eat Last*, great leaders create environments where people feel safe enough to take risks, speak truth, and grow.

Influence built on fear is temporary. Influence built on trust is timeless.

True leadership is emotional stewardship — guiding the energy of others toward a shared vision.

---

**Modern Examples of EQ Leadership**

**1. Jacinda Ardern — Compassion in Crisis**

During the 2019 Christchurch tragedy, New Zealand's Prime Minister didn't just govern — she comforted a nation. Her calm empathy unified people across faiths and backgrounds.

**2. Ratan Tata — Leading with Heart**

When Tata Group acquired Jaguar Land Rover, he prioritized employee morale and cultural respect. His empathy rebuilt trust and turned losses into profits.

**3. Indra Nooyi — Leading with Listening**

The former PepsiCo CEO wrote personal letters to the parents of her senior executives, thanking them for raising great leaders. That emotional touch deepened loyalty across the organization.

These leaders prove that emotional intelligence is not a "soft" skill — it's *strategic empathy* in action.

**Reflection Questions**

1. How do I make others feel in my presence — calm, inspired, or tense?
2. When conflict arises, do I react or respond with understanding?
3. How often do I listen to understand rather than to reply?
4. What could I do this week to build more trust and emotional safety in my relationships or team?

---

**Affirmations for Relational Intelligence**

- I lead with empathy, authenticity, and purpose.
- I listen deeply and communicate with compassion.
- My presence calms, inspires, and uplifts others.
- I create emotional safety wherever I go.

---

**Practical Action Steps**

1. **Empathy Practice:** Once a day, ask someone, "How are you feeling?" — and *truly* listen.
2. **Feedback Ritual:** Invite honest feedback from a peer or team member about your communication style.
3. **Energy Awareness:** Before meetings, check your emotional state — calm your energy before you enter the room.
4. **Conflict Reframing:** During your next disagreement, focus on understanding before defending.

5. **Gratitude Expression:** Appreciate one person daily — gratitude strengthens emotional bonds.

---

**Closing Thoughts: The Heart of Leadership**

At its core, emotional intelligence is not about being nice — it's about being *real*.

It's about understanding that leadership is not just what you do; it's who you are when people need you most.

Your intelligence may open doors. Your emotional intelligence keeps them open.

When you master both — inner awareness and outer connection — you become unstoppable: calm in chaos, compassionate in conflict, and courageous in growth.

That's what the world needs — leaders who lead from the heart, not just the head.

# CHAPTER 7: THE POWER OF VISUALIZATION AND MIND PROGRAMMING

# PART 1: THE SCIENCE OF VISUALIZATION — HOW THE BRAIN CREATES REALITY

## Seeing It Before You See It

Everything begins twice: first in your mind, then in reality.

Every invention, every achievement, every transformation you admire — started as a vision.
Airplanes, smartphones, skyscrapers, music, art, businesses — none existed until someone imagined them vividly enough to make them real.

Visualization is not daydreaming. It's *mental rehearsal for success.*

Your mind cannot distinguish vividly imagined experiences from real ones. When you visualize something with emotional intensity, your brain fires the same neural circuits as if you were living it. Over time, these neural pathways strengthen, training your subconscious to believe — and act — as if the vision is already true.

That's how the greatest achievers program their reality before it even happens.

---

### The Brain's Secret: Neuroplasticity

Until a few decades ago, scientists believed the brain was static — fixed after childhood. Today, we know that's false.

Your brain is *neuroplastic*, meaning it continuously rewires itself based on thoughts, experiences, and emotions.

Every thought you repeat forms a neural connection. Repeated thoughts build networks. Networks become habits. Habits shape identity.

Visualization accelerates this process by creating a powerful inner simulation — like mental training for your goals.

Olympic athletes use visualization as part of their daily routine. Studies at the University of Chicago found that basketball players who *only visualized* practicing free throws improved almost as much as those who physically practiced.

Your mind rehearses success before your body performs it.

That's not magic — that's neuroscience.

---

**The Reticular Activating System (RAS): Your Mind's GPS**

Have you ever noticed that when you buy a new car, you suddenly start seeing it everywhere? That's your **Reticular Activating System** (RAS) in action.

The RAS is a network of neurons in your brainstem that filters information. It decides what deserves your attention and what doesn't. Out of millions of sensory inputs every second, it lets through only what aligns with your focus and beliefs.

When you set a clear intention and visualize it repeatedly, your RAS starts spotting opportunities that align with that vision.

It's not that the opportunities weren't there before — you just weren't tuned to notice them.

Visualization tunes your mental frequency to the "channel" of your goals.

If you constantly visualize failure, your RAS finds evidence of failure.
If you visualize success, it filters in people, ideas, and resources that move you toward it.

You don't attract by chance — you align by choice.

---

**The Subconscious Mind: Your Inner Operating System**

Think of your subconscious as the world's most loyal employee — it executes every command you give it without judgment.

But it doesn't respond to logic; it responds to *emotion and repetition.*

When you visualize with emotion — joy, gratitude, confidence — your subconscious accepts that image as truth and begins aligning your behavior accordingly.

That's why elite performers visualize in sensory detail:

- What they see, hear, feel, smell, and even taste in their moment of success.
- The emotions of accomplishment.
- The gratitude of "already having it."

The subconscious begins reprogramming your identity to match the outcome.

And identity determines destiny.

If you repeatedly visualize yourself as calm, capable, and successful, your subconscious starts guiding your choices — consciously and unconsciously — toward that version of you.

That's the foundation of **mind programming.**

---

### Visualization vs. Affirmation: The Perfect Pair

Affirmations feed the subconscious through *words.*
Visualization feeds it through *images.*

Together, they're unstoppable.

Affirmations like "I am confident and focused" rewire your linguistic pathways. Visualization makes those affirmations *visceral.*

Imagine you have a big presentation tomorrow. You can affirm, "I am calm, confident, and clear," while simultaneously visualizing yourself standing tall, speaking with clarity, hearing applause, and feeling satisfaction.

The combination of thought (affirmation) and imagery (visualization) embeds deep neural conditioning.

Over time, your brain normalizes that version of you.

You stop *trying* to be confident — you *become* it.

### The Science of Mirror Neurons and Mental Rehearsal

When you watch someone perform an action — a musician playing, a speaker presenting, a runner sprinting — your brain activates **mirror neurons**, as if you were performing the action yourself.

That's why visualization is so effective: your brain rehearses success internally.

Top athletes call this *mental imagery training.*
They visualize every detail — the tension of the muscles, the rhythm of breathing, the feeling of victory.

Michael Phelps, the Olympic swimmer, used visualization before every race. He imagined each stroke, each turn, each sensation in water. When his goggles filled with water during a championship final, he still won — because he had rehearsed that scenario in his mind thousands of times.

He didn't panic; he performed.

Visualization trains the brain for performance under pressure.

---

**The Emotional Factor: Feel It to Make It Real**

Emotion is the amplifier of visualization.

A mental picture without emotion is just a daydream. A vision charged with emotion becomes a command to your subconscious.

When you *feel* the joy, gratitude, and confidence of already living your goal, your brain releases dopamine and serotonin — the same chemicals of achievement and fulfillment.

That emotional chemistry tells your subconscious, "This is real."

The more vividly and emotionally you imagine, the more your brain encodes it as reality.

The formula is simple:

**Intensity + Repetition + Emotion = Reprogramming.**

---

**How to Practice Effective Visualization**

Here's a step-by-step method I use and teach:

**Step 1: Relax Your Mind**

Sit quietly, close your eyes, and take slow, deep breaths. Relax your body. The goal is to quiet the analytical mind so the subconscious becomes receptive.

**Step 2: Define the Vision Clearly**

Be specific. "I want success" is vague. "I see myself confidently delivering a keynote presentation to 500 people, inspiring them deeply, and feeling proud and fulfilled" is powerful.

**Step 3: Engage All Senses**

See the room, the colors, the people's faces. Hear your voice and their applause. Feel the warmth, the confidence, the air on your skin. The more sensory detail, the stronger the imprint.

**Step 4: Add Emotion**

Feel gratitude as if it's already happened. Smile. Let joy flood your body. This is the emotional glue that seals the vision into your subconscious.

**Step 5: Anchor the Feeling**

As you feel success, touch your heart, breathe deeply, or press your thumb and finger together. Over time, this physical cue will instantly reconnect you with that state of confidence.

**Step 6: Repeat Daily**

Morning and night — when the subconscious is most open — visualize for 5–10 minutes. Repetition builds familiarity, and familiarity creates belief.

**Step 7: Take Inspired Action**

Visualization without action is fantasy. Action without vision is chaos. Together, they create alignment.

---

**Visualization in Daily Life**

Visualization isn't limited to grand goals — it applies to everyday success.

Before an important meeting, visualize it going smoothly.
Before a workout, visualize yourself finishing strong.
Before a difficult conversation, visualize calm, clarity, and resolution.

Your brain rehearses the desired outcome, reducing anxiety and increasing performance.

Even small daily visualizations accumulate power over time.

That's how mental focus becomes momentum.

---

**Reprogramming Limiting Beliefs**

Visualization isn't just about creating new realities — it's also about dissolving old mental barriers.

Your mind might carry unconscious programs like:

- "I'm not good enough."
- "Success is for others, not me."
- "Money is hard to earn."

These beliefs sabotage growth because your subconscious always acts in accordance with what it believes to be true.

Visualization helps you override these outdated programs by replacing them with new mental images that represent success, abundance, and worthiness.

When you visualize repeatedly, your subconscious updates its "self-image." And as Maxwell Maltz taught in *Psycho-Cybernetics*, self-image determines performance.

You will never outperform your self-image — but you can reprogram it.

---

### Case Study: Visualization in Sports and Business

**Sports Example:**
When NBA legend Kobe Bryant trained under coach Tim Grover, he visualized every possible scenario of the game — even missed shots, fouls, and pressure moments — until his mind became immune to fear.

He once said, *"If you've seen it in your mind, it can't surprise you in real life."*

**Business Example:**
Sara Blakely, founder of Spanx, visualized her company's success before it existed. Every day, she saw herself on Oprah, selling her product to millions. Years later, that visualization manifested — exactly as imagined.

Their secret wasn't luck — it was mental rehearsal plus relentless action.

---

### Why Visualization Works for Leaders and Professionals

Visualization enhances three core leadership abilities:

1. **Focus:** Clarifies priorities and strengthens attention.
2. **Confidence:** Prepares the mind emotionally for high-stakes situations.
3. **Creativity:** Opens neural networks that generate innovative ideas.

Leaders like Steve Jobs and Walt Disney were master visualizers. They didn't just see what was — they saw what could be.

Disney once said, *"If you can dream it, you can do it."* He visualized Disneyland years before it was built, walking through imaginary streets and rides in his mind until it became real.

That's leadership through imagination — and neuroscience validates it.

### Avoiding Common Visualization Mistakes

Many people visualize incorrectly. Here's how to avoid the traps:

- **Mistake 1: Visualizing from lack.**
  Thinking "I want money" affirms "I don't have it." Instead, visualize *already having abundance.*

- **Mistake 2: Being vague.**
  Your brain needs clear pictures. "Success" is too abstract; define what it looks and feels like.

- **Mistake 3: Over-controlling outcomes.**
  Visualize the essence, not every detail. Allow flexibility for better results than you imagined.

- **Mistake 4: Neglecting emotion.**
  The subconscious responds to *feeling*, not just imagery.

When visualization is done right — with belief, clarity, and emotion — it becomes a force of creation.

---

**Reflection Questions**

1. What mental images dominate my thinking — success or struggle?
2. How clearly can I see my ideal future in sensory detail?
3. What limiting beliefs still shape my subconscious "self-image"?
4. How can I use visualization daily to reinforce confidence and focus?

---

**Affirmations for Mental Reprogramming**

- I create my reality through the power of my focused mind.
- My vision is clear, vivid, and already unfolding.
- I see myself confident, abundant, and at peace — and so it is.
- Every thought I focus on expands into my life.

---

**Practical Action Steps**

1. **Morning Visualization:** Spend 5 minutes visualizing your day going perfectly — smooth meetings, confidence, productivity, gratitude.
2. **Goal Movie:** Create a vision board or short video with images of your goals, set to uplifting music. Watch it daily.
3. **Emotion Anchor:** When you visualize, attach a gesture (hand over heart, deep breath). Use it before real challenges to recall your empowered state.

4. **Self-Image Upgrade:** Each night, visualize your "Future Self"— confident, composed, successful — living the life you're building.

# CHAPTER 7: THE POWER OF VISUALIZATION AND MIND PROGRAMMING

## PART 2: THE SPIRITUAL DIMENSION — THE UNIVERSAL LAW OF MIND AND ENERGY

### The Energy Behind Thought

Everything in the universe is energy — vibrating at different frequencies. Your body, your thoughts, your emotions, your words — all emit energy.

Quantum physics teaches that the observer influences the observed. In simple terms: **your consciousness shapes your reality.**

What you consistently think and feel sends out a frequency — and that frequency attracts experiences that match it.

This is the deeper truth behind visualization and mind programming. It's not only mental training; it's energetic alignment.

When your thoughts, emotions, and beliefs vibrate in harmony with your desires, life begins to reorganize itself in your favor.
When they vibrate in conflict — fear, doubt, resistance — life reflects that, too.

You're not fighting for your dreams; you're *tuning into them.*

---

### The Law of Vibration and Attraction

Long before "The Secret" made it mainstream, ancient teachings spoke of this principle.

The **Law of Vibration** states that everything — including your thoughts — is energy moving at a frequency.

The **Law of Attraction** is the natural consequence: energy of a certain frequency attracts similar energy.

When you visualize with belief and gratitude, you raise your vibration to the level of your desired reality. That vibration becomes a magnet.

This isn't about wishful thinking — it's about alignment.

If you want abundance but constantly think about lack, your vibration says, "I don't have."
If you want love but dwell on loneliness, your frequency says, "I'm unworthy."
If you want success but fear failure, your signal says, "I'm uncertain."

The universe doesn't respond to your words — it responds to your *frequency.*

So the question is: what frequency are you broadcasting?

---

**The Power of Belief: Faith as Creative Energy**

Faith is not a concept — it's a creative vibration.

When you believe something is possible, that belief alters your energy field. You start acting, speaking, and deciding from confidence instead of doubt.

The universe mirrors that conviction.

Every major spiritual tradition echoes this truth:

"According to your faith, it will be done unto you." — Matthew 9:29
"What you seek is seeking you." — Rumi
"The mind is everything. What you think, you become." — Buddha

Belief is the bridge between the unseen and the seen.

Visualization without belief is like sending a signal with no power. Visualization with faith is a transmission that the universe can't ignore.

That's why combining visualization with deep inner conviction turns intention into manifestation.

---

**Gratitude: The Accelerator of Manifestation**

Gratitude is the highest frequency of all — the vibration of abundance and sufficiency.

When you visualize your dreams *and feel grateful as if they've already happened*, you align with the energy of having, not wanting.

Gratitude tells the universe, "I already have it within me."
And the universe says, "Then let me show you more of it."

This principle is not mystical — it's energetic psychology.

When you're grateful, your brain releases serotonin and dopamine — chemicals of joy and satisfaction. These reinforce positive expectation and draw experiences that match your emotional state.

Gratitude turns visualization into magnetism.

Start every visualization by saying,

"Thank you for this vision already being true."

That single phrase aligns your heart and mind in the vibration of fulfillment.

---

**Imagination: The Creative Portal**

Imagination is not fantasy — it's *spiritual technology.*

When you imagine, you tap into a higher field of consciousness — the creative matrix of the universe. You access possibilities that don't yet exist in physical form.

Einstein, one of the most logical minds in history, understood this profoundly. He said:

"Imagination is everything. It is the preview of life's coming attractions."

What he meant is that imagination accesses a higher dimension of potential — a field where all realities already exist as energetic blueprints.

When you visualize, you select the blueprint you wish to experience and bring it into focus.
Through belief, gratitude, and emotion, you download it into your physical life.

Your imagination is your direct connection to the infinite.

---

**The Heart-Mind Coherence**

Modern research from the HeartMath Institute reveals something astonishing:
The heart generates an electromagnetic field 60 times stronger than the brain's.

When you align the mind's intention with the heart's emotion — logic with love, vision with gratitude — your energy becomes coherent and powerful.

This state, called **heart-brain coherence**, increases intuition, clarity, and synchronicity.

In practical terms:

- The *mind* creates the image.

- The *heart* energizes it with emotion.
- Together, they broadcast a frequency that reorganizes reality.

That's why the most effective visualization begins with feeling gratitude or love — emotions that open the heart. Once the heart is open, the mind's picture becomes a command to the universe.

You're no longer forcing reality — you're flowing with it.

**Synchronicity: The Language of the Universe**

When your vibration matches your vision, life starts to whisper back through synchronicities — meaningful coincidences that guide your path.

You think of someone, and they call.
You visualize an opportunity, and it shows up.
You imagine a solution, and suddenly it appears in conversation or a book.

These aren't random; they're confirmations that you're aligned with your intention.

Synchronicity is the universe's feedback system — its way of saying, "Yes, you're on the right track."

Instead of doubting these signs, acknowledge them with gratitude. That recognition strengthens the frequency further.

The more you trust these nudges, the more they multiply.

---

**Overcoming Energetic Resistance**

Sometimes visualization feels like it's not working.
You're imagining, affirming, believing — but results seem slow.

This usually happens when there's **energetic resistance** — subconscious fear, doubt, or attachment to how the outcome should unfold.

You can't attract from a state of tension. You must release control and trust divine timing.

The universe doesn't respond to neediness; it responds to *certainty.*

Here's a powerful mindset shift:

"I trust that what's meant for me cannot miss me."

When you release the need for control, you free your energy. That surrender creates space for miracles.

Sometimes not getting what you want immediately is protection — alignment takes time.

Faith isn't believing everything will happen your way.
Faith is knowing that whatever happens will lead you closer to truth.

---

**Visualization as Co-Creation**

Visualization is not about manipulating reality — it's about collaborating with it.

You're a co-creator with the universe. You hold half the equation: *intention*. The universe holds the other half: *timing and orchestration.*

When you visualize clearly and act decisively, you send your order. The universe responds in perfect timing.

Your job is to stay aligned — in thought, emotion, and faith.

This partnership is ancient. Mystics call it "manifestation." Scientists call it "observation." Leaders call it "vision."

But the principle is the same:
**You become the frequency of your future — and your future finds you.**

---

**Real-Life Stories of Spiritual Visualization**

**1. Jim Carrey — The $10 Million Check**

Before fame, Jim Carrey wrote himself a check for $10 million for "acting services rendered," dated five years in the future. He visualized holding it, feeling it, and thanking the universe daily.
Five years later — to the exact date — he earned $10 million for his role in *Dumb and Dumber.*

**2. Oprah Winfrey — Vision with Intention**

Oprah credits visualization and gratitude as her guiding forces. She once said,

"You don't get what you want — you get what you believe."
She visualized her role in *The Color Purple* so clearly that when she received the offer, she said, "I had already seen it happen."

**3. Arnold Schwarzenegger — Mental Movie**

Before becoming a Hollywood star, he visualized success every day. "I saw myself in the movies. I saw the lights, the cameras, the interviews. I didn't just dream it — I *lived* it in my mind until it became reality."

Each of them used visualization not as fantasy, but as faith in motion.

---

**The Three Levels of Manifestation**

Visualization operates at three energetic levels:

1. **Mental Level — Thought**
   You form clear mental images of what you desire.

2. **Emotional Level — Feeling**
   You infuse those images with gratitude and joy.

3. **Energetic Level — Vibration**
   You sustain the feeling long enough for it to magnetize opportunities.

When these three align — thought, feeling, and vibration — creation becomes inevitable.

You no longer chase. You attract.

---

**Daily Spiritual Visualization Practice**

Try this 10-minute ritual each morning:

1. **Still the Mind**
   Breathe deeply and let thoughts settle. Feel your body relax.

2. **Open the Heart**
   Think of one thing you're deeply grateful for. Let gratitude fill your chest.

3. **Visualize Your Future**
   See your dream as already real. Imagine it in vivid detail — the environment, people, success, peace.

4. **Feel It Fully**
   Smile. Breathe the emotion of accomplishment. Feel that vibration radiate from your heart.

5. **Say Thank You**
   Whisper "Thank you for this reality now unfolding."

6. **Release and Trust**
   Let go. Go live your day, confident that the unseen is working in your favor.

This daily alignment creates spiritual coherence—the state where mind, heart, and energy flow as one.

---

**Reflection Questions**

1. What energy am I consistently radiating — fear or faith, doubt or gratitude?
2. How can I bring more feeling and belief into my visualizations?
3. What signs or synchronicities have I noticed that confirm alignment with my goals?
4. Where might I still be resisting or trying to control outcomes instead of trusting the process?

---

**Affirmations for Spiritual Alignment**

- I am a powerful co-creator with the universe.
- My thoughts, emotions, and energy attract my highest good.
- I release all resistance and trust divine timing.
- Gratitude opens every door meant for me.

---

**Practical Action Steps**

1. **Morning Alignment Ritual:** Begin your day with gratitude and visualization.
2. **Vibration Audit:** Throughout the day, notice your energy — uplift it through music, nature, or affirmations.
3. **Trust Practice:** When something doesn't go as planned, affirm, *"This too is guiding me."*
4. **Synchronicity Journal:** Write down coincidences and positive signs — evidence strengthens faith.

---

**Closing Thoughts: Vision Is Creation**

You are not just a thinker — you are a creator.

Every thought is a brushstroke on the canvas of your destiny.
Every emotion is the color that gives it life.
Every belief is the architecture of what will unfold.

When science and spirit merge — when you visualize with focus *and* faith — you become unstoppable.

The universe doesn't respond to effort; it responds to *alignment.*
And when your inner world vibrates with certainty, peace, and gratitude—your outer world rearranges itself to match it.

You don't need to chase your dreams — you need to *become* them.

That is the true power of visualization and mind programming.

# CHAPTER 8: OVERCOMING FEAR AND BUILDING UNSHAKABLE CONFIDENCE

## PART 1: UNDERSTANDING FEAR

### The Silent Thief of Dreams

Every human being — no matter how accomplished — has felt fear.

Fear of failing. Fear of being judged. Fear of losing control. Fear of not being enough.

Fear is universal. It's the silent thief that robs us of courage before we even take the first step.

But here's the truth: fear itself isn't the enemy — our *relationship* with fear is.

Most people try to escape fear, suppress it, or deny it. Yet the secret to confidence is not the absence of fear; it's learning to walk with it.

When you understand fear — when you face it, listen to it, and master it— it transforms from an obstacle into your greatest ally.

Fear isn't here to stop you. It's here to *shape* you.

---

### What Fear Really Is

Let's demystify fear.

From a scientific perspective, fear is a natural biological response — your body's built-in alarm system. The moment your brain perceives a threat, real or imagined, your **amygdala** (the brain's fear center) activates.

It floods your body with **adrenaline and cortisol**, sharpening your senses and preparing you to fight, flee, or freeze.

This response once kept our ancestors alive on the savannah. But in modern life, that same system gets triggered by emails, deadlines, or public speaking — things that aren't life-threatening, yet feel emotionally dangerous.

The brain doesn't distinguish between physical danger and psychological threat. That's why you feel the same pounding heart before a presentation as a caveman did when facing a tiger.

But here's the key insight:

Fear is not a sign that you're weak. It's a sign that you're expanding.

Whenever you step into the unknown — growth, risk, visibility — fear appears. It's proof that you're crossing a threshold.

Fear, therefore, is not your foe. It's a compass.
It points directly to where your growth lies.

---

**The Two Types of Fear**

There are two kinds of fear:

1. **Survival Fear** – The kind that protects you from real danger.
   It's healthy and necessary.
   Example: stepping away from a speeding car or avoiding a dark alley at midnight.

2. **Psychological Fear** – The imagined kind that holds you back from progress.
   Example: fear of failure, rejection, or being seen.

Survival fear keeps you alive.
Psychological fear keeps you *small*.

And because the brain's wiring treats both as equally real, you must learn to consciously reprogram your responses to the second kind.

You can't eliminate fear — but you can train your mind not to bow to it.

---

**The Illusion of Limitation**

Every fear you carry has one root cause: **the illusion of limitation.**

Fear whispers, *"You can't."*
Confidence whispers back, *"Watch me."*

Fear magnifies what could go wrong. Confidence expands what could go right.

Most of your fears are mental projections — not facts. Studies show that **over 85% of what we worry about never happens**. And of the remaining 15%, most situations turn out better than expected or teach valuable lessons.

That means fear lies most of the time.

Fear imagines the worst version of the future and convinces you it's real.

But once you shine awareness on fear, it loses its grip.

---

**How Fear Manipulates the Mind**

Fear uses subtle tricks to keep you stuck.

1. **The Voice of Doubt:**
   "What if I fail?"
   "Who am I to do this?"
   "People will laugh."

Fear disguises itself as self-doubt — logical, cautious, protective. But beneath it lies insecurity, not wisdom.

2. **The Trap of Perfectionism:**
   Fear says, "Wait until it's perfect."
   Perfectionism is procrastination wearing a suit.

3. **The Illusion of Control:**
   Fear convinces you that by delaying or overplanning, you can avoid pain.
   But the longer you wait, the smaller your courage becomes.

Recognizing these patterns is step one in reclaiming your power.

---

**Courage Is Not the Absence of Fear**

Let me tell you a secret that all courageous people know:
They feel fear — every single time.

Nelson Mandela, who faced decades of imprisonment, once said,

"I learned that courage was not the absence of fear, but the triumph over it."

Courage means acting *despite* fear — not waiting for it to disappear.

Every time you act while afraid, you prove to yourself that fear can't stop you. That proof builds self-trust. And self-trust is the foundation of confidence.

---

**Transforming Fear into Fuel**

You can't outrun fear — but you can **transmute** it.

Here's how:

**1. Name It**

The first step in mastering fear is identifying it clearly.
When you name fear, you separate from it.
Say, "I feel anxious about this presentation," instead of "I am anxious."

**2. Reframe It**

Ask yourself:

"What is this fear trying to protect me from?"
Often, it's trying to prevent pain or embarrassment.
Thank it — then tell it, "I can handle this."

**3. Breathe Through It**

Fear tightens your body. Deep breathing loosens its grip.
Try this: inhale slowly for 4 counts, hold for 4, exhale for 6.
This activates your parasympathetic system — your inner calm.

**4. Take Small Action**

Action shrinks fear.
Each step you take sends evidence to your brain: *I am capable.*

As psychologist Susan Jeffers wrote, *"Feel the fear and do it anyway."*

The antidote to fear isn't avoidance — it's action.

---

**The Inner Dialogue of Fear vs. Confidence**

Your inner voice can either be your greatest ally or your fiercest critic.

Fear says:

"What if I fail?"
Confidence says:
"What if I learn and grow?"

Fear says:

"I'm not ready."
Confidence says:
"I'll never be fully ready — and that's okay."

Fear says:

"People will judge me."
Confidence says:
"They'll judge anyway — I might as well be authentic."

Rewriting your inner dialogue is one of the most powerful confidence tools you possess.

Your subconscious listens to your words — and builds your reality accordingly.

---

**The Physiology of Courage**

When fear strikes, it's not just mental — it's physical. Your body tenses, heart rate spikes, palms sweat.

But courage has its own physiology too — and you can train it.

Try this **"Power Posture"** technique validated by social psychologist Amy Cuddy's research:

- Stand tall.
- Open your chest.
- Place your hands on your hips.
- Take two deep breaths.

After just two minutes, testosterone (confidence hormone) rises and cortisol (stress hormone) drops.

Your body posture signals safety to your brain, which begins producing chemicals of calm.

This is how you *physically embody confidence* before your mind catches up.

---

**From Fear to Flow**

When you focus too much on fear, your brain's threat system dominates.
When you focus on purpose, curiosity, and service, the **prefrontal cortex** — your higher reasoning center — takes control.

That's when fear fades and *flow* begins.

Flow is the state of deep presence where action feels effortless and time disappears.
It's the state athletes, artists, and innovators tap into — and you can too.

You enter flow when your focus shifts from "What if I fail?" to "What can I create right now?"

Fear looks inward. Flow looks outward.

You can't be fearful and fully present at the same time.

Presence dissolves fear.

---

**Case Study: The Fear Breakthrough**

When I coached a young professional named Meera, she was terrified of public speaking. Every time she had to present, her heart raced, her voice trembled, and she'd lose her train of thought.

We didn't start with techniques. We started with understanding her fear. She realized her fear wasn't of speaking — it was of *being judged.*

Once she acknowledged that, we practiced small exposures:

- Speaking for one minute in meetings.
- Breathing deeply before standing up.
- Visualizing applause instead of criticism.

Within months, her fear transformed into energy. She began to channel that adrenaline into excitement.

Today, she leads quarterly presentations for hundreds — and says, *"I still feel fear, but now I ride it like a wave."*

That's emotional mastery in action.

---

**The Fear-Confidence Cycle**

Here's the paradox: you don't wait for confidence to act.
You act to build confidence.

Every time you do something fearful, your comfort zone expands. The unknown becomes known, and your brain updates its safety map.

Confidence is not built in silence. It's built in discomfort.

The formula is simple:

**Action → Evidence → Confidence → More Action.**

Confidence isn't gifted — it's *earned through experience.*

---

**Fear and the Ego**

At its core, fear is the ego's defense mechanism — the mind's attempt to protect its identity.

The ego fears rejection because it craves approval. It fears failure because it equates worth with performance.

But the moment you realize your worth is *inherent*, fear loses power.

You are not your mistakes.
You are not your titles.
You are the awareness behind all experience — calm, infinite, unbreakable.

When you identify with that deeper self, the ego's fears shrink into background noise.

That's true confidence — not arrogance, but anchored self-assurance.

---

**Reflection Questions**

1. What fear has been holding me back the most recently — and what might it be trying to teach me?
2. How does fear show up in my body, and how can I breathe through it consciously?
3. In what ways might I be confusing fear with intuition?
4. What's one small, courageous action I can take this week to stretch my comfort zone?

---

**Affirmations for Courage**

- Fear is a signal of my growth, not my weakness.
- I breathe through fear and act with purpose.
- Every time I face fear, I grow stronger and freer.
- My courage expands faster than my doubt.

---

**Practical Action Steps**

1. **Fear Journal:** Write down your biggest fears, then list the evidence against them. Challenge their logic.
2. **Courage Ladder:** Break a scary goal into micro-steps. Celebrate each step.
3. **Breath Practice:** Before any stressful moment, do three rounds of slow 4-4-6 breathing.
4. **Body Power Pose:** Before meetings, stand tall for two minutes and affirm, "I am ready."

5. **Courage Ritual:** End each day by noting one fear you faced — no matter how small.

# CHAPTER 8: OVERCOMING FEAR AND BUILDING UNSHAKABLE CONFIDENCE

## PART 2: BUILDING UNSHAKABLE CONFIDENCE

### Confidence: The Energy of Self-Belief

Confidence isn't arrogance. It isn't pretending to be fearless.

True confidence is quiet. Grounded. It's the calm assurance that no matter what happens — you can handle it.

It's not built on achievements or titles; those can be taken away. Real confidence is internal — the steady trust that *you are capable, worthy, and enough.*

You don't wait for confidence to begin. You build it by beginning.

Confidence is the reward of action repeated until competence emerges.

---

### The Psychology of Confidence

At its core, confidence is a combination of two beliefs:

1. **Self-Efficacy** — "I can do this."
2. **Self-Worth** — "I deserve success."

When both align, you radiate confidence effortlessly.

People often focus only on skills (self-efficacy), but neglect the deeper belief (self-worth). That's why some high achievers still feel like impostors — because they haven't anchored their worth beyond performance.

To build unshakable confidence, you must strengthen both: *the skill and the self.*

---

**The Confidence Loop**

Confidence grows in a loop of four steps:

1. **Action** — You take a step despite fear.
2. **Experience** — You survive, learn, and adapt.
3. **Evidence** — You prove to your brain that you're capable.
4. **Belief** — You begin to trust yourself more.

Then the cycle repeats — stronger each time.

You don't become confident by waiting. You become confident by *doing*.

---

**From Comparison to Competence**

One of the fastest ways to destroy confidence is comparison.

When you measure your worth by others' progress, you disconnect from your own journey.

Confidence doesn't come from being *better* than others — it comes from being *better than you were yesterday.*

Shift your focus from **comparison** to **competence**.

Ask:

"What's one skill I can improve by 1% today?"

Confidence built on growth is unshakable because it doesn't depend on applause — it depends on progress.

**The Inner Language of Confidence**

Your self-talk determines your self-trust.

If you constantly say, "I can't," "I'm not good enough," or "What if I fai l?"— your subconscious listens.

Words create reality.
Change your inner dialogue, and you change your energy.

Instead of saying "I can't," say "I'm learning how."
Instead of "I've never done this," say "This is an opportunity to grow."
Instead of "I'm nervous," say "I'm excited."

Your brain interprets the same physiological signals (heart racing, adrenaline) differently based on language. Nervousness reframed as excitement becomes fuel.

That's emotional alchemy.

---

**Confidence Through Preparation**

Nothing builds confidence like preparation.

When you prepare thoroughly, you calm your nervous system and earn self-trust.

Whether it's a presentation, interview, or negotiation — preparation transforms anxiety into anticipation.

Preparation says, "I respect this moment enough to be ready."

But here's the secret: over-preparation can become procrastination.

The goal isn't perfection — it's readiness.
You don't need to know everything. You need to trust yourself to adapt.

Confidence is preparation plus presence.

**Body Language: The Outer Expression of Inner Belief**

Your body speaks before you do.

Studies show that over **70% of communication is nonverbal.**

Confident body language projects trust even before words are spoken.

Key principles:

- **Posture:** Stand tall, shoulders open, spine straight.
- **Eye Contact:** Look at people, not through them — warm, steady, and genuine.
- **Gestures:** Use open palms and controlled movements.
- **Voice:** Slow, clear, and deliberate.

These signals don't just influence others — they influence *you.*

When you act confidently, your brain releases hormones that make you *feel* confident.

Confidence is both a cause and an effect.

---

**Authenticity: The Core of Real Confidence**

You can't fake true confidence — because real confidence isn't performance; it's *presence.*

Authenticity means showing up as yourself, without pretending or apologizing for it.

When you stop trying to impress and start trying to *express*, people feel your sincerity — and you feel your freedom.

Authenticity eliminates the pressure of perfection.

When you're authentic, you don't need to remember your mask. You just *be*.

Confidence born from authenticity is the most magnetic kind — because it's rooted in truth.

---

**Confidence in Communication**

Confidence and communication go hand in hand.

How you express yourself determines how others perceive your value.

To speak confidently:

1. **Breathe before you speak.**
   Calm breath = calm voice.

2. **Pause often.**
   Silence signals composure, not weakness.

3. **Use storytelling.**
   People remember stories more than data.

4. **Own your space.**
   Don't shrink physically or verbally.

5. **Speak from service.**
   Instead of "What will they think of me?" ask "How can I help them?"

When you shift from self-focus to service-focus, anxiety dissolves.

Because fear thrives on self-centeredness — "me, me, me." Confidence thrives on contribution — "How can I add value?"

---

**Confidence in Leadership**

Leadership without confidence is chaos.

A confident leader doesn't need to dominate — they inspire through clarity, consistency, and calm.

People follow confidence because it provides safety.

But the key is *humble confidence* — strength without arrogance.

The confident leader says:

"I don't have all the answers, but I'll figure it out."

They admit mistakes, seek feedback, and lead with authenticity.

Confidence without empathy becomes ego.
Confidence with empathy becomes influence.

---

**Overcoming Impostor Syndrome**

Even high achievers battle a quiet enemy: *impostor syndrome.*

That voice that whispers, "You don't belong here," "You just got lucky," "They'll find out you're not good enough."

But impostor syndrome only exists in people who *actually care* about excellence.

The way to dissolve it is through truth:

- You're not lucky — you're prepared.
- You're not faking it — you're growing into it.
- You belong because you showed up, and you're learning.

Confidence grows not from perfection, but from progress under pressure.

You can't fake experience — but you can accumulate it.

---

### The Power of Self-Integrity

Confidence is built every time you keep a promise to yourself.

When you say, "I'll wake up early," and you do — trust grows.
When you say, "I'll speak up," and you do — courage grows.
When you say, "I'll follow through," and you do — belief grows.

Self-integrity compounds into self-trust, and self-trust becomes confidence.

Every time you act in alignment with your word, your subconscious whispers,

"I can count on me."

That's unshakable confidence.

---

### Confidence in Action: Everyday Practices

Here are daily ways to embody confidence in real life:

1. **The Mirror Exercise:**
   Each morning, look at yourself and say, "I trust you. You can handle anything today."
   It may feel awkward at first — that's proof it's working.

2. **The "1% Bolder" Rule:**
   Each day, do one small thing slightly bolder than yesterday.
   Over time, these micro-risks compound.

3. **The "As If" Principle:**
   Act as if you already are the person you want to become — confident, capable, and calm. Behavior rewires belief.

4. **Celebrate Wins:**
   Every evening, write down three things you did well today. Confidence grows through acknowledgment.

5. **Speak Up Once a Day:**
   Share an idea, ask a question, or voice an opinion — even if it's scary. Each act builds your confidence muscle.

---

**Modern Examples of Unshakable Confidence**

**1. Serena Williams — Confidence Through Consistency**

She doesn't wait for external validation. Her confidence comes from years of disciplined preparation.
As she once said, *"I've always believed I was the best, even when I wasn't."*

**2. Dwayne "The Rock" Johnson — Confidence Through Authenticity**

He turned vulnerability into connection by openly sharing his failures, anxiety, and growth journey. Confidence isn't hiding pain — it's owning your truth.

**3. Malala Yousafzai — Confidence Through Purpose**

Shot for pursuing education, she continued speaking globally with grace and courage. Her confidence wasn't ego-driven; it was mission-driven.

These examples prove: real confidence isn't loud. It's powerful, peaceful, and purposeful.

### The Spiritual Side of Confidence

Confidence is not just mental; it's energetic.

When your mind, body, and spirit align — when you know your worth and trust the flow of life — you radiate calm certainty.

Confidence doesn't say, "I can control everything."
It says, "Whatever happens, I'll find my way."

Faith is the root of confidence.

When you trust that life supports your growth, every challenge becomes a lesson, not a threat.

Confidence, therefore, is an act of surrender — to your own power, to your purpose, and to the wisdom of the universe.

---

**Reflection Questions**

1. What area of my life needs more confidence right now — and what small action can I take to build it?
2. When do I feel most authentic and powerful — and how can I bring that energy into other areas?
3. How can I reframe self-doubt into self-trust?
4. What promises do I need to start keeping to myself again?

---

**Affirmations for Confidence**

- I trust myself completely in every situation.
- I am calm, capable, and confident under pressure.
- My actions create proof of my power.
- I radiate authenticity and strength.
- I was born to express, not to impress.

---

**Practical Action Steps**

1. **Preparation Ritual:** Before any key event, take five deep breaths, smile, and say, "I am ready."
2. **Confidence Journal:** Record daily victories — no matter how small.
3. **Voice Training:** Practice speaking slower and with intention for five minutes each day.

4. **Environment Upgrade:** Surround yourself with people who celebrate courage, not perfection.

5. **Monthly Fear Challenge:** Once a month, do something outside your comfort zone.

---

**Closing Thoughts: Confidence Is a Choice**

Confidence is not something you're born with — it's something you *build*.

Every act of courage, every kept promise, every honest word strengthens it.

Fear asks, "What if I fall?"
Confidence replies, "What if I fly?"

And every time you take a leap — even a small one — you rise closer to the person you were always meant to be.

The world doesn't need more perfect people. It needs more *confidently imperfect* ones — people who show up fully, love deeply, and lead boldly.

Because when you believe in yourself — truly, deeply — the universe mirrors that belief right back to you.

# CHAPTER 9: PURPOSE, PASSION, AND PEAK PERFORMANCE

## The Search for Meaning in a High-Speed World

We live in an age of constant motion.
Emails never stop. Targets keep shifting. Technology changes faster than our thoughts can catch up.
And in this relentless pace, one quiet question echoes in the background of every ambitious soul:

"Why am I really doing all this?"

I've met countless young professionals and leaders who are brilliant, capable, and driven — yet quietly restless. They hit milestones that should make them happy, but something feels incomplete.
That "something" is not a lack of success; it's a lack of **alignment**.

Purpose is the compass that makes achievement meaningful.
Without it, even victory feels hollow.

When you rediscover *why* you do what you do, life transforms from a treadmill into a trajectory.

---

### Rediscovering Your Why — The Foundation of True Success

Purpose isn't a distant, mystical concept. It's not hiding in some secret mountain retreat or buried in a self-help book. It already lives inside you — in your curiosities, your pains, your joys, and your values.

Think back to moments that made you feel most alive.
When did you lose track of time because you were fully immersed?
What topics light up your energy when you speak?
What injustice stirs you to act?

Those clues reveal your *why.*

When I mentor young leaders, I often ask, "If you could do something for the world and never get paid, what would it be?"
That question disarms the ego and exposes the heart.

Your purpose is where your **strengths meet service** — the intersection between what you're good at and what the world needs.

Purpose isn't found; it's *remembered*.

---

**Purpose Fuels Passion**

When you're clear about why you're doing something, your passion ignites naturally.

Passion is energy — the fire that makes effort feel like play.
But passion without purpose burns out; purpose without passion fades into duty.

Together, they create unstoppable momentum.

When you know your "why," every "how" becomes easier.
Challenges become meaningful. Work becomes worship.

Even fatigue feels different when it's in the service of something that matters.

As Friedrich Nietzsche wrote,

"He who has a why to live can bear almost any how."

---

### Turning Meaning into Motivation

Purpose gives direction; passion gives drive. But to convert them into motion, you need motivation — the daily spark that transforms inspiration into action.

There are two kinds of motivation:

1. **External Motivation** — recognition, rewards, praise.
2. **Internal Motivation** — joy, mastery, contribution.

External motivation fades quickly. Internal motivation is renewable.

When you're driven by contribution instead of competition, energy multiplies.
Instead of asking, "What can I get?" ask, "What can I give?"

This shift changes everything.
The former fuels anxiety; the latter fuels excellence.

---

### The Science of Flow — Where Purpose Meets Performance

Have you ever been so absorbed in work that time vanished? That's **flow** — the peak state of human performance identified by psychologist Mihaly Csikszentmihalyi.

In flow, your skills match the challenge perfectly. You feel stretched, but not stressed; focused, but not forced.

Purpose triggers flow because it aligns challenge with meaning.
When your goals matter to you, concentration becomes effortless.

Athletes call it being "in the zone."
Artists call it "creative trance."
I call it "presence with purpose."

Flow isn't just enjoyable — it's measurable.
Research shows people in flow are **five times more productive** and report **three times higher satisfaction**.

That's what happens when passion and purpose merge into performance.

---

### Discipline — The Bridge Between Goals and Greatness

Passion gives you energy to start; discipline keeps you going when energy fades.

Every purpose-driven person eventually meets the wall of monotony — those days when excitement dips and distractions rise.

Discipline is love in action.
It's the daily choice to honor your vision, even when no one's watching.

Discipline isn't about punishment; it's about alignment.

When your habits reflect your values, consistency becomes natural.
You stop forcing progress and start flowing toward it.

Remember:

Motivation gets you moving.
Discipline keeps you growing.

---

### Energy Management — The Hidden Key to Peak Performance

Peak performance isn't just about working harder; it's about managing energy wisely.

Your body and mind are an ecosystem — physical, emotional, and spiritual energy must be balanced to sustain excellence.

Here's a framework I teach:

1. **Physical Energy —** Sleep, nutrition, movement.
   - Sleep is not laziness; it's recovery.
   - Move daily; motion creates emotion.
2. **Emotional Energy —** Relationships, gratitude, joy.
   - Connect deeply; isolation drains.
   - Gratitude transforms stress into strength.
3. **Mental Energy —** Focus and mindset.
   - Practice dopamine detox, as we discussed earlier.
   - Schedule deep-work hours free from digital noise.
4. **Spiritual Energy —** Purpose and presence.
   - Begin each day with intention; end with reflection.

When energy is balanced, performance feels effortless.

---

**Modern Stories of Purposeful Performance**

**Elon Musk — Obsession with a Mission**

Whatever your opinion of him, one truth is clear: Musk's energy comes from mission, not money. He works 16-hour days not for wealth, but for an interplanetary vision. That's purpose in overdrive.

**Kobe Bryant — The Mamba Mindset**

After losing a crucial NBA game, Bryant was seen at the gym at 4 a.m. the next morning. His passion for mastery wasn't conditional on victory — it was fueled by the love of becoming better.

**Marie Forleo — Purpose Through Service**

From dance to digital entrepreneurship, Marie built her brand on helping others realize "Everything is figureoutable." Her purpose: to empower belief. Her performance flows from that mission.

Each story reminds us: when meaning drives action, greatness follows naturally.

**Integrating Purpose into Daily Life**

Purpose isn't only for grand moments; it's for ordinary days.

You can live purposefully in every role — professional, parent, student, or friend — by asking one simple question:

"How can I add value here?"

Purpose is not a destination; it's a daily decision.
Even small acts done with intention create massive impact over time.

---

**The Alignment Equation**

Purpose × Passion × Performance = Fulfillment.

When one variable is missing, life feels off-balance.

- Purpose without passion feels like obligation.
- Passion without purpose feels like chaos.
- Performance without either feels like exhaustion.

But when all three align, you move from success to significance.

That's the sweet spot — the state where work becomes worship and growth becomes gratitude.

**Reflection Questions**

1. What activities make me feel most alive and aligned?
2. How can I bring more meaning into my current work or studies?
3. What daily practices help me sustain energy and focus?
4. Where am I performing without passion, or passionate without purpose — and how can I realign?

---

**Affirmations for Purposeful Living**

- I live and lead with clear intention every day.
- My passion is the expression of my purpose.
- I perform at my peak because I am aligned, not pressured.
- My work serves something greater than myself.
- I am energized, focused, and fulfilled.

---

**Daily Practices for Peak Living**

1. **Morning Intention:** Begin each day by asking, "What kind of impact do I want to create today?"
2. **Flow Hour:** Schedule one hour daily for deep, meaningful work.
3. **Passion Recharge:** Engage in one activity each week purely for joy — no agenda.
4. **Purpose Review:** Every Sunday, journal about how your actions aligned with your values.

5. **Gratitude Wind-Down:** End each day naming three ways you expressed purpose or passion.

---

**Closing Thoughts: Living With Purposeful Power**

Purpose gives your life direction.
Passion gives it momentum.
Performance gives it expression.

When the three merge, you stop chasing success and start *embodying* it.

You become a force of nature — calm yet unstoppable.

Because you're no longer motivated by fear of failure or hunger for approval. You're driven by contribution, creation, and connection.

That's the highest form of living — not survival, not even success, but **significance.**

So let this be your mantra as you move forward:

"I live with purpose, I act with passion, and I perform with presence."

That's how you awaken the unstoppable you.

# CHAPTER 10: RESILIENCE — RISING STRONGER FROM EVERY FALL

## The Strength Hidden in Struggle

No matter who you are — student, entrepreneur, or CEO — life will test you.
You will face rejection, failure, heartbreak, and unexpected detours.
But here's what separates the broken from the unbreakable: **resilience.**

Resilience is not about avoiding pain; it's about *transforming through it.*
It's the ability to bend without breaking, to stumble but still move forward.

We often believe strong people are those who never fall.
But in truth, the strongest are those who fall, learn, rise, and keep walking — wiser, humbler, stronger than before.

Resilience is not a gift. It's a skill — built through adversity, reflection, and perseverance.

---

### What Resilience Really Means

The word *resilience* comes from the Latin *resilire*, meaning "to leap back."
But I believe real resilience goes beyond bouncing back — it's about *bouncing forward*.

You don't return to who you were before the fall; you evolve into someone wiser because of it.

Resilience is the fusion of three inner powers:

1. **Acceptance** — facing reality with courage.

2. **Adaptability** — responding creatively to change.

3. **Agency** — taking ownership of your next step.

When you embody these, no storm can sink you — it can only reshape your path.

---

### The Psychology of Resilience

From a neuroscience perspective, resilience is the brain's ability to regulate stress and recover from setbacks. When challenges arise, your amygdala triggers the fight-flight-freeze response. But resilient individuals activate the **prefrontal cortex** — the rational part of the brain — faster.

In simple terms: they pause, breathe, and reframe.

They don't suppress emotion; they process it and choose a constructive response.

Resilience isn't about never feeling pain — it's about not letting pain define you.

---

### The Art of Acceptance

One of the hardest truths in life is that pain is inevitable — but suffering is optional.

Suffering begins when we resist what already is.
Acceptance, on the other hand, doesn't mean giving up; it means saying,

"This happened. Now, what can I learn from it?"

When you accept reality, your energy shifts from resistance to resolution.
You stop asking, "Why me?" and start asking, "What now?"

That question alone can change everything.

---

**From Breakdown to Breakthrough**

I once coached a senior executive who had just lost his job after 20 years in the same company. He was devastated — his identity and self-worth were tied to that position.

For weeks, he spiraled into anger and disbelief.
But when we reframed the event — not as a failure, but as feedback — something shifted.

He realized that the layoff wasn't a punishment; it was a push toward reinvention.

Within a year, he launched his own consulting firm. Today, he says losing that job was "the best thing that ever happened to me."

That's resilience: the ability to turn pain into purpose.

---

**The Growth Mindset: Your Inner Shield**

Psychologist Carol Dweck introduced a concept that underpins all resilience — the **growth mindset.**

A fixed mindset says:

"I failed, therefore I'm a failure."

A growth mindset says:

"I failed, therefore I learned."

Resilient people don't define themselves by outcomes. They see every experience as data — a chance to improve.

They understand that life is not a test to pass; it's a game to grow through.

When you adopt this mindset, failure loses its sting.

---

**Emotional Mastery: Resilience from Within**

Resilient people don't avoid emotions; they manage them consciously. They allow sadness, anger, or fear to pass *through* them — not *stay within* them.

Here's a quick framework: **Pause, Process, Proceed.**

1. **Pause:** When you're triggered, stop reacting immediately.
2. **Process:** Name the feeling — "I feel disappointed" — without judgment.
3. **Proceed:** Choose a response that aligns with your values.

This creates space between stimulus and response — the space where strength lives.

---

**The Power of Perspective**

When adversity hits, your greatest weapon is perspective.

You can see the fall as failure — or as foundation.

Imagine a seed buried in darkness. From the outside, it looks like destruction. But underground, it's transformation.
The soil that seems to bury it is actually preparing it to grow.

That's what happens to us in life.
Sometimes the universe buries us so we can bloom stronger roots.

Resilience begins when you trust that every challenge carries a hidden gift.

---

**Stories of Unbreakable Spirit**

**1. J.K. Rowling — From Rejection to Revelation**

Before *Harry Potter*, Rowling was a struggling single mother living on welfare. She faced **12 publisher rejections** before one said yes.
Her resilience wasn't in persistence alone — it was in belief.
She once said, *"Rock bottom became the solid foundation on which I rebuilt my life."*

**2. Nick Vujicic — The Power of Acceptance**

Born without arms or legs, Nick could have lived in despair. Instead, he built a global motivational movement, reminding millions that *"If you can't get a miracle, become one."*

**3. Nelson Mandela — Strength in Forgiveness**

After 27 years in prison, Mandela emerged not bitter, but better. His resilience was rooted in forgiveness — the courage to choose peace over revenge.

Each of these people transformed pain into purpose.
Their stories prove that resilience is not in avoiding difficulty — it's in discovering who you are *because of it.*

---

**The Resilience Equation**

Resilience = Response – Resistance

Your response to adversity matters more than the adversity itself.
The greater your resistance ("This shouldn't happen"), the greater your suffering.
The more flexible your response ("This is tough, but I'll adapt"), the faster you recover.

You can't control every event — but you can always control your *energy toward it.*

---

**Physical and Mental Practices to Build Resilience**

Resilience isn't just mental — it's physical, emotional, and spiritual training combined.

1. **Build a Strong Body:** Exercise releases endorphins and lowers stress hormones.
2. **Prioritize Sleep:** Your brain repairs emotional circuits during deep rest.
3. **Practice Mindfulness:** Daily meditation rewires neural pathways for calm.
4. **Connect with People:** Social support accelerates recovery from stress.
5. **Keep a Gratitude Journal:** It trains your brain to notice progress instead of problems.

Small habits compound into inner strength.

**Spiritual Resilience — Trusting the Process**

Beyond mindset and science lies something deeper — *faith.*

Faith doesn't mean blind belief; it means trusting the bigger picture even when the details hurt.

Resilient people understand that life is happening *for* them, not *to* them.
They find meaning even in chaos.

When everything falls apart, faith whispers,

"This, too, shall pass. And when it does, you'll see why it happened."

Resilience without faith is effort.
Resilience with faith is peace.

---

**From Recovery to Reinvention**

Every setback gives you two choices: rebuild what was, or reinvent what can be.

The most resilient people don't just recover; they reimagine.
They ask:

"What version of me is this challenge trying to create?"

Maybe failure isn't rejection — maybe it's redirection.
Maybe endings are invitations to evolve.

Resilience is not about returning to normal — it's about creating a *new normal.*

---

**Reflection Questions**

1. What was one challenge that once broke me but later built me?
2. How do I typically respond to setbacks — with resistance or resourcefulness?
3. What daily habits can strengthen my emotional and physical resilience?
4. Where in my life do I need to stop "bouncing back" and start "bouncing forward"?

---

**Affirmations for Strength**

- I rise stronger every time life tests me.
- I am unshakable because I adapt and evolve.
- I trust the process, even when I don't understand it.
- Every setback is setting me up for growth.
- My spirit bends, but never breaks.

---

**Practical Action Steps**

1. **Resilience Journal:** Each week, note one challenge and how you overcame it. Revisit these entries to build evidence of strength.
2. **Daily Reset:** When stressed, pause, breathe deeply, and reframe the situation.

3. **Micro-Challenges:** Do something slightly uncomfortable daily to expand tolerance for discomfort.
4. **Gratitude Habit:** End each day naming three small wins or lessons learned.
5. **Faith Reminder:** Keep a quote or mantra nearby — something that anchors you in hope during chaos.

---

**Closing Thoughts: The Beauty of Rising Again**

Falling is part of the human experience.
But staying down is a choice.

Life will test you not to break you — but to reveal how strong you already are.

Resilience is not the absence of struggle; it's the presence of *spirit.*
It's what turns wounds into wisdom, scars into stories, and pain into power.

So when life knocks you down — smile, breathe, and rise.
Because every rise after a fall deepens your character and expands your capacity.

You are not fragile — you are forged.
You are not broken — you are being built.

And when you rise again, as you always will, the world will see what you were truly made of: **resilient fire.**

# CHAPTER 11: THE ART OF LETTING GO AND MOVING FORWARD

## The Weight We Carry

We all carry invisible weight — disappointments, betrayals, regrets, or expectations that didn't go as planned.
We tell ourselves we've "moved on," but inside, we keep replaying the old scenes like broken records:

"If only I had done that differently..."
"Why did they treat me that way?"
"What if things had worked out?"

The truth is, you can't walk freely into your future if you're still chained to your past.
Letting go is not weakness — it's *liberation.*

It's not about forgetting what happened; it's about releasing the emotional grip it has on you.

Every moment you spend in resentment or regret drains the energy you need for creation and growth.
Letting go is how you reclaim your power.

---

## Understanding Why We Hold On

Letting go sounds simple — until it's personal.
We cling to people, situations, and identities for one main reason: **fear.**

- Fear of loss: *"What if I never find better?"*
- Fear of guilt: *"Maybe it was my fault."*
- Fear of uncertainty: *"Who will I be without this?"*

The ego wants control and certainty. It would rather hold on to pain than face the unknown.
But freedom requires surrender — the courage to trust life beyond what you can control.

Holding on doesn't keep you safe; it keeps you *stuck*.

---

**The Illusion of Control**

We spend so much energy trying to control outcomes, people, and timelines — believing that if we just try harder, we can make life obey our expectations.

But control is an illusion.
You can influence, prepare, and plan — but you can never dictate.

Life unfolds through both your choices *and* forces beyond your control.
Peace comes when you learn to master effort, not outcomes.

True power lies not in controlling everything — but in trusting yourself to handle *anything*.

As I often remind my mentees:

"You can't always control what happens, but you can always control what happens next."

---

**Forgiveness — The Ultimate Act of Freedom**

Forgiveness is one of the most misunderstood concepts in personal growth.

Forgiving doesn't mean condoning the wrong.
It means refusing to let the pain poison your future.

When you hold resentment, you're not punishing the other person — you're imprisoning yourself.

Anger is like holding a hot coal and waiting for someone else to burn.

Forgiveness is dropping that coal.
It's saying, *"I choose peace over poison."*

You forgive not because they deserve it — but because *you do.*

---

**Letting Go of the Past Version of Yourself**

Sometimes, the hardest person to forgive is yourself.

We replay our mistakes, relationships, and missed chances — punishing ourselves for being human.

But you cannot heal if you keep condemning the version of you that didn't know better.
That person was doing the best they could with the awareness they had.

The goal of growth isn't to hate your past self — it's to love them for surviving.

Letting go means honoring your evolution.
Every version of you was a stepping stone toward wisdom.

So today, whisper to yourself:

"I release the need to be perfect. I honor my journey, and I move forward with compassion."

---

**Detachment — The Spiritual Side of Letting Go**

Detachment doesn't mean apathy; it means emotional clarity.

It's the ability to engage fully without clinging desperately.

When you practice detachment, you stop seeking security in things outside yourself — achievements, people, or possessions.

You understand that everything in life is temporary — including emotions, pain, and success.

That realization brings peace.

Detachment allows you to love more freely, work more creatively, and live more fully — because your happiness is no longer hostage to outcomes.

---

**The Process of Letting Go**

Letting go isn't a one-time event — it's a process.
Here's a framework I often share with my clients and readers:

**1. Acknowledge**

Admit what you're holding onto — whether it's a person, mistake, or dream that ended.
Naming the attachment is the first step to loosening it.

**2. Feel**

Don't rush to "get over it." Allow the emotions to move through you — sadness, anger, guilt, grief.
Emotion is energy in motion. When you feel it, you free it.

**3. Learn**

Ask, *"What was this experience here to teach me?"*
Lessons transform pain into wisdom.

**4. Release**

Write a letter you'll never send. Meditate, cry, talk — do whatever symbolizes release for you.
Say aloud, *"I am ready to let this go."*

**5. Replace**

Fill the space with something new — purpose, hobbies, people, peace. Letting go is not losing something; it's making room for better things to enter.

---

**Real-Life Stories of Letting Go**

**1. Steve Jobs — Letting Go to Leap Forward**

In 1985, Steve Jobs was fired from Apple — the company he co-founded. It was humiliating and painful.
But years later, he said it was the best thing that happened to him. It freed him to enter one of the most creative periods of his life, leading to Pixar and the rebirth of Apple itself.
Sometimes, losing something opens the door to everything.

**2. Maya Angelou — Letting Go of Anger**

After years of trauma, Maya Angelou turned pain into poetry. Her resilience came from forgiveness and perspective. She wrote, *"I can be changed by what happens to me. But I refuse to be reduced by it."*

**3. Relationships That Ended**

Many people discover their strength not when they hold on, but when they finally release what's no longer aligned.
Letting go of toxic relationships isn't loss — it's self-respect.

---

### The Science of Release

Modern psychology supports what ancient wisdom taught: letting go heals both mind and body.

- Studies from Harvard show that practicing forgiveness reduces stress and lowers blood pressure.
- Mindfulness-based therapy helps reduce emotional rumination by strengthening the brain's "default mode network," improving emotional regulation.
- Neuroscience confirms that emotional release — through journaling, therapy, or meditation — rewires the brain's reward centers, creating peace.

Letting go literally changes your chemistry.

---

### Letting Go of Control and Embracing Flow

When you release control, you invite flow.

Flow happens when you're present — not past-obsessed or future-anxious.

Letting go means trusting the process — allowing life to unfold in its own divine rhythm.

As you stop forcing outcomes, opportunities start appearing organically.
You become receptive instead of resistant.

Remember this:

"The tighter you grip, the faster it slips. The more you trust, the more it flows."

**Moving Forward with Grace**

Moving forward doesn't mean you forget what happened — it means you integrate it.
You carry the lesson, not the luggage.

Every ending creates space for a beginning.
Every goodbye is a doorway to growth.

Moving forward is not about rushing — it's about rebuilding with intention.

Start small:

- One new habit that inspires joy.
- One conversation that feels authentic.
- One goal that aligns with your purpose.

Momentum is medicine.

The universe rewards movement — even imperfect steps forward.

---

**Reflection Questions**

1. What situation or memory am I still holding onto emotionally?
2. What am I afraid will happen if I truly let it go?
3. What lesson has this experience taught me about myself?
4. What can I begin doing today to move forward with peace and purpose?

---

**Affirmations for Release and Renewal**

- I release the past and trust the flow of life.
- I forgive myself and others, freeing my heart from old pain.
- I am at peace with what was and excited for what's coming.
- I let go of control and embrace divine timing.
- I am whole, complete, and ready to move forward.

---

**Practical Action Steps**

1. **Closure Letter:** Write to your past — a person, version of yourself, or dream — and express gratitude, forgiveness, and release.
2. **Symbolic Ritual:** Burn the letter safely or tear it, saying aloud, "I release this with love."
3. **Daily Let-Go Practice:** At the end of each day, mentally release any frustration or disappointment before sleep.

4. **Declutter Your Space:** Physical clutter mirrors emotional clutter — clear both.
5. **Focus Reset:** Choose one new goal aligned with your present values.

---

**Closing Thoughts: The Freedom of Release**

Letting go is not the end — it's the beginning of peace.

It's how you make space for new blessings, people, and possibilities.

When you release the grip of the past, you open your hands to receive the future.
You stop chasing closure — because you *become* it.

The art of letting go is the art of living lightly — trusting that every ending hides a higher design.

You are not what you lost.
You are what you've learned, loved, and become because of it.

So breathe, forgive, release — and step forward.
Because your next chapter is waiting, and it needs the *free* version of you.

---

# CHAPTER 12: BECOMING LIMITLESS — THE EVOLUTION OF THE UNSTOPPABLE YOU

## The Journey So Far

If you've made it to this point, pause for a moment.
Take a deep breath.

You've walked through courage, clarity, focus, faith, discipline, emotion, resilience, and renewal.
You've learned how to build habits, face fear, master your mind, and trust your heart.

That's not just reading — that's evolution.

This book was never about becoming someone new; it's about *remembering who you already are*.
The limitless version of you has always existed — beneath the layers of fear, doubt, and conditioning.

Now, we strip away the final layer: limitation itself.

---

### What It Means to Be Limitless

Limitless doesn't mean you can do *everything*.
It means you can rise above *anything*.

It's not about superhuman perfection — it's about human potential, fully activated.

Being limitless is a mindset — a state of expansion where you no longer ask,

"Can I?"
but instead affirm,
"How can I?"

It's the quiet conviction that whatever life throws your way, you'll adapt, grow, and find a way forward.

Limitless people aren't the ones who have no obstacles — they're the ones who no longer see obstacles as limits.

---

**Breaking the Barriers of Belief**

Every limitation starts as a belief.

Before any wall exists outside you, it exists in your mind.
And here's the liberating truth — beliefs can be rewritten.

Ask yourself:

- What have I been told is impossible?
- Who told me I couldn't?
- And why did I believe them?

The most powerful moment in your life is when you stop accepting other people's limits as your reality.

History is full of people who broke barriers simply because they didn't know they "couldn't."
They saw opportunity where others saw obstacle.
They saw potential where others saw peril.

Their secret? They believed differently — and then acted accordingly.

**The Inner Expansion**

To become limitless, you must expand three dimensions of yourself:

1. **Mind Expansion** — Learning, curiosity, and unlearning old patterns.
2. **Heart Expansion** — Compassion, empathy, gratitude, and self-love.
3. **Spirit Expansion** — Connection to something larger than yourself — purpose, consciousness, the divine.

Each layer amplifies the others.
When your mind is open, your heart softens.
When your heart opens, your spirit rises.
When your spirit rises, you realize — there were never any walls, only doors you hadn't opened yet.

---

**The Limitless Mind**

The mind is your greatest ally — or your greatest cage.
It becomes limitless when you master three keys:

**1. Curiosity Over Certainty**

Replace "I know" with "I'm learning."
Certainty closes doors; curiosity opens them.

**2. Possibility Thinking**

Ask expansive questions:

- "What else could this mean?"
- "What's another way to solve this?"
- "Who can I become through this?"

Your brain expands in the direction of your questions.

### 3. Lifelong Learning

Read, listen, explore.
Growth is the oxygen of a limitless life.
Every new skill, idea, or challenge stretches the edges of your comfort zone — until limitation no longer fits you.

---

### The Limitless Heart

The heart is the emotional compass of your power.
When it's blocked by fear, resentment, or ego, your energy stagnates.

But when it's open — to love, gratitude, and forgiveness — everything flows.

To live from the limitless heart:

- **Forgive freely.** Holding grudges anchors you to the past.
- **Love deeply.** Vulnerability is not weakness; it's strength in pure form.
- **Practice gratitude.** It magnetizes more of what you value.
- **Serve others.** Service turns success into significance.

A limitless heart doesn't seek to conquer others — it seeks to connect, uplift, and understand.

That's the highest vibration of power.

---

### The Limitless Spirit

Your spirit is the eternal part of you — the quiet observer beneath all thoughts, titles, and achievements.

When you connect to that awareness, you stop identifying with momentary struggles.
You realize: you are not the storm; you are the sky that holds it.

To live from this space is to move with deep peace and trust.

Meditation, stillness, or prayer aren't just spiritual practices — they are tuning mechanisms for clarity.
They remind you that the universe isn't against you; it's collaborating *through* you.

Being limitless spiritually means surrendering the need to force and allowing flow to guide your path.

---

**The Power of Self-Trust**

All limitless living begins with one foundation: **trust yourself.**

You've already survived 100% of your hardest days. You've learned, healed, and adapted.
Every scar on your soul is proof of resilience.

When you truly trust yourself, fear loses its authority.

You stop seeking validation and start leading from conviction.

Self-trust is built through consistency — showing up daily for your goals, your growth, your integrity.
Each time you honor your word, you whisper to your subconscious, *"I've got this."*

That whisper becomes your roar.

---

**Turning Vision into Expansion**

Limitless people are vision-driven, not circumstance-driven. They don't wait for perfect conditions; they create them.

Every breakthrough begins as a bold decision:

"I'm done playing small."

The moment you declare that, life starts testing your declaration — not to punish you, but to prepare you.

Obstacles aren't signs you're off track — they're signs you're leveling up.

Remember: diamonds aren't made in comfort; they're forged under pressure.

Your pressure is shaping your power.

---

**Stories of Limitless Transformation**

**1. Elon Musk — Redefining Possibility**

From near bankruptcy at SpaceX to revolutionizing space travel, Musk's story proves that vision backed by persistence can rewrite reality itself.

**2. Oprah Winfrey — Turning Pain into Power**

Abuse, poverty, and rejection didn't define her — purpose did. She once said, *"Turn your wounds into wisdom."* That's limitless thinking embodied.

**3. Roger Bannister — The Four-Minute Barrier**

Experts said no human could run a mile in under four minutes. In 1954, Bannister did — and within a year, dozens followed.
Once one mind breaks a limit, collective consciousness expands.

Your personal breakthroughs will do the same — not just for you, but for everyone watching.

---

**From Self-Mastery to Contribution**

The ultimate expression of being limitless isn't power — it's purpose.

When you rise, lift others.
When you learn, teach.
When you grow, guide.

True evolution is not about ego; it's about impact.

The unstoppable you doesn't chase applause — it creates ripples of transformation.

Your presence becomes your message.

---

**Integration: Living the Limitless Blueprint**

Here's how to integrate everything you've learned in this journey:

1. **Mindset:** Reframe fear into feedback.
2. **Habits:** Build systems, not just goals.
3. **Emotion:** Feel fully, but don't get stuck.
4. **Discipline:** Show up even when it's hard.
5. **Purpose:** Align your actions with meaning.
6. **Faith:** Trust the unseen process.
7. **Service:** Uplift others as you rise.

This is not a one-time transformation — it's a lifelong evolution.

**Reflection Questions**

1. Where in my life am I still thinking small or doubting my power?
2. What would I attempt if I knew I could not fail?
3. How can I use my gifts to serve and elevate others?
4. What daily rituals keep me connected to my limitless state?

---

**Affirmations for Limitless Living**

- I am infinite potential in human form.
- Every challenge strengthens my purpose.
- I trust my path and flow with divine timing.
- I create, inspire, and uplift effortlessly.
- I am the unstoppable force of my own evolution.

---

**Practical Action Steps**

1. **Vision Reset:** Write a one-year vision as if everything went right. Read it daily.
2. **Limit Audit:** Identify three limiting beliefs — and rewrite them as empowering truths.
3. **Contribution Habit:** Do one small act of service every week — anonymously if possible.
4. **Expansion Hour:** Dedicate 60 minutes weekly to learning or creating something new.

5. **Gratitude Meditation:** Each night, visualize your future self thanking you for today's effort.

---

**Closing Thoughts: You Are the Evolution**

There will never be a final version of you — only a next one.

Growth is infinite, and so are you.

Every time you rise after a fall, choose faith over fear, or act on purpose—you expand what's possible for yourself and everyone around you.

That's what it means to be **unstoppable** — not that nothing can break you, but that nothing can *keep you broken.*

So go forward, not as a seeker anymore, but as a creator — designing your destiny with clarity, courage, and compassion.

The world doesn't need another follower of fear.
It needs another leader of light.

And that leader is you.

---

## Epilogue: The Awakening

As you close this book, remember — this isn't the end of your journey.
It's the moment your new one begins.

The world will still challenge you, tempt you, and test your faith. But now, you carry tools that no challenge can take away: Vision. Focus. Faith. Discipline. Resilience. Love.

You have awakened the unstoppable you — the version that leads with purpose, lives with passion, and performs with peace.

Your mission now is simple:
**Live what you've learned. Share what you've become. Inspire others to awaken too.**

Because when one person rises, humanity rises with them.

---

✨ ***You are limitless. You are light. You are unstoppable.*** ✨